LIFE
Lessons
COLLEGE
Failed
TO TEACH
You

Thandi,
To your health,
happiness,
and money
moves!
-Baylie R

LIFE
Lessons
COLLEGE
Failed
TO TEACH
You

BAYLIE ROBINSON

Dedication

To all of the new adults who feel lost and are still searching for their purpose in life. This book is dedicated to us.

To my parents, Mark and Theresa. Y'all are one badass pair and I'm the fiery Baylie I am today because of you both! With that said, there's a few pages in here you both should probably skip over!

Contents

Introduction

My name is Baylie Robinson, not Baylie Rockefeller. If I were the other BR this would be a very different book. Instead, this book is about trying to navigate the real world after college. Unfortunately, that degree you have is only part of your story. The balance has yet to be written and boy, are you in for a rude awakening. Luckily, I'm here to make your awakening a little less rude. I promise I'm not going to judge you. You can think of me as the brutally honest friend you've known for years. I'm the college graduate who is willing to share my own unfiltered experiences, even when they don't showcase me in the best light.

WHY AM I QUALIFIED TO WRITE THIS BOOK?

Not too long ago, I was standing in your shoes. I graduated college at the age of twenty and I had no idea what I was getting myself into. I had to learn everything the hard way. Within My first three years after graduation I had:

- Moved a total of 5,000 miles

- Been demoted

- Been promoted three times

- A mental breakdown

- Interviewed for over 15 positions

- Received eight job offers

- Quit two jobs

- Improved my relationship with my parents

- Been wrongfully fired

- Received unemployment benefits

- Endured aimless dating app dates

- Reported to nine different managers

- Narrowed my friend circle

- Lost my six-year-old dog to cancer

- Moved to my dream city

- Paid off a whopping $2,747 of my $26,843 student loan debt

WHO AM I?

I guess you can say I'm quite the vocal individual. I played basketball for eight years on the same all-girls team and was best friends with the coach's daughter. After winning first place in our division way too many times, our coach realized we weren't being challenged enough and enrolled us in the all-boys division. As a 12-year-old girl, you can imagine the level of concern the team parents had. Before our first game, one of the boys on the opposing team told me "Go back home and play with your collection of dolls." I replied, "Go back inside your mother!"

I've always been a go-getter. If I wanted something, I made a plan to get it. No one could stop me. Figuring out what I wanted to do was the first part of the battle. The second part was figuring out how the hell to survive adulthood. Throughout my life, my goals and aspirations have changed, but my spirit and the core of my personality have not.

For years I wanted to be an attorney. I genuinely loved to argue as child. I loved proving my point and being right. Even if I was wrong, I found a way to twist things to at least be "less wrong" than the other person. My parents would get calls at home from teachers not because I was bad, but because I talked too much. I'd get moved into different seats away from certain individuals and then would end up making friends with the new person next to me.

I wasn't an A student like my Cornell graduate parents. I was average. I was not the kid who got an A on a test without studying. If I had friends, weekend plans, and maintained a B average, I was happy. This mentality followed me into college. During college, I realized that law school was a requirement if I wanted to be an attorney. The idea of an additional three years of school after college was a deal breaker for me. I could see myself as an attorney, as many others, but could not see myself going into another three years of assignments, all-night studying sessions, and exams. I did what many other college students did and went into a business program, like my father. It wasn't until my second year of college when I realized that fashion was something I wanted to pursue. After completing two internships, one at a local boutique and the other in Nordstrom's buying office, and receiving a job offer six months prior to graduation, I knew I wanted to create a career in corporate retail. It was the perfect blend of finance, relationship building, merchandising, and buying products.

On average, there are 1.8 million college graduates a year. Each of these 1.8 million graduates spend an average of $23,000 a year at their designated university, taking classes such as business law and Calculus. How many of these graduates were fully prepared for the real-world post college graduation? There's no class that teaches students about corporate politics or the fact that in most states an employer can legally fire an employee for no reason at all. No one warned these students that their father would try and collect a year's worth of their phone bill or that they'd receive a student loan bill six months post-graduation for $460 a month on an entry-level salary. In the figure below, you can see a breakdown about student loan debt and some of the surprising post-college expenses no one warns you about.

FIGURE 1

According to the U.S. Federal Reserve and
Federal Reserve Bank of New York, here is a
general picture of the student loan landscape:

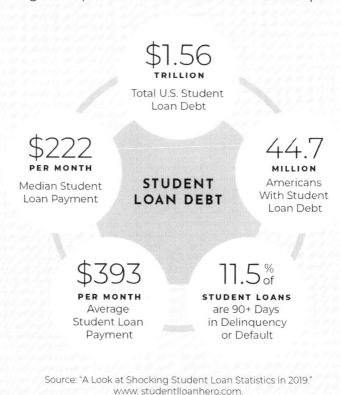

$1.56
TRILLION
Total U.S. Student
Loan Debt

$222
PER MONTH
Median Student
Loan Payment

STUDENT
LOAN DEBT

44.7
MILLION
Americans
With Student
Loan Debt

$393
PER MONTH
Average
Student Loan
Payment

11.5%
of
STUDENT LOANS
are 90+ Days
in Delinquency
or Default

Source: "A Look at Shocking Student Loan Statistics in 2019."
www. studentlloanhero.com.

These are real life issues that college graduates are facing with no
preparation. This is why you are holding this book in your hands.

WHO IS THIS BOOK FOR?

Life Lessons College Failed to Teach You is the primer I wish
I'd had when I graduated. Whether you're a parent trying to

understand what your post-college, 20-something child is going through, a recent college grad, a teacher, a counselor, or a person five years into your career, this book is for you.

Life Lessons College Failed to Teach You is structured into 11 chapters. Each section contains personal anecdotes, hard statistics, and even a few visual aids because we all love a book with pictures! Every chapter within these three sections will conclude with a lessons learned summary in relation to the topic.

WHAT WILL THIS BOOK DO FOR YOU?

· You will learn how to be more professional.

· You will learn how to answer interview questions, find a mentor, search for a job search, quit a job, and navigate corporate politics.

· You will learn how to navigate your personal life.

· You will understand the importance of dating (or the lack thereof), finding a roommate, and eliminating toxic people from your life.

· You will learn how to self-reflect.

While I share many experiences from my own life, there will be several activities that will help get you closer to identifying where your happiness is.

Now, let's get started.

PART ONE:

Navigating Work Life

CHAPTER ONE

Your First Job: The Entryway to Chained Freedom

"Just remember during your dark times that no difficulty can discourage, no obstacle dismay, no trouble dishearten the man [or woman] who has acquired the art of being alive. Difficulties are but dares of fate, obstacles but hurdles to try his [or her] skill, troubles but bitter tonics to give him [or her] strength; and he [or she] rises higher and looms greater after each encounter with adversity."

—Ella Wheeler Wilcox

It's college graduation day and the moment you've been waiting for, let alone screaming for, is finally here. Some of your friends have no job prospects, no idea what they're going to do, and will probably move back in with mom and dad. (Sorry, English, Liberal Arts, and Philosophy majors. You should have known this would happen).

A handful of your friends probably think the last six months with their supposed end-of-college fling or booty call will turn into something more serious. These people have decided to follow their "significant other" to a new city or state. The rest of your friends had enough sense to secure an internship in between their drunken rollercoaster of a semester and ended up getting a job offer. I fell into this latter bucket. This orange juice drinking, humidity prone, sunscreen wearing, umbrella using Floridian was moving to Seattle, Washington. It was the farthest state, with the exception of Alaska, I could have ever moved to. I had two weeks after graduation to get my life together before my January start date. To be honest, I wasn't excited at all. Yes, it was a once-in-a-lifetime opportunity that most people in my field would kill for. I was a Business Management major with an emphasis on Retail Merchandising. I secured a position in a merchant training program at the buying office for Nordstrom, a multi-billion-dollar luxury retailer. I spent two months in Seattle during my internship and knew Seattle wasn't for me two weeks after being there. Although I loved the company and the job when I moved there, I knew it wouldn't be permanent. So why did I move there if I didn't want to in the first place?

I HAD NO BETTER OFFER.

The figure below will give you a better idea of why I (and many other recent college graduates!) chose to take a less-than-ideal job based on the current job market.

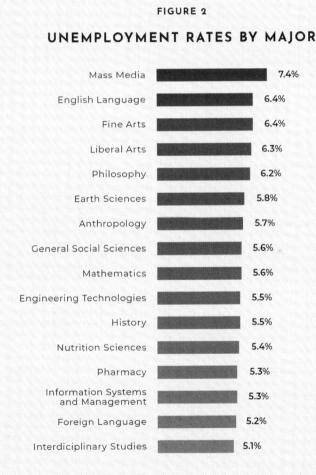

FIGURE 2

UNEMPLOYMENT RATES BY MAJOR

Mass Media	7.4%
English Language	6.4%
Fine Arts	6.4%
Liberal Arts	6.3%
Philosophy	6.2%
Earth Sciences	5.8%
Anthropology	5.7%
General Social Sciences	5.6%
Mathematics	5.6%
Engineering Technologies	5.5%
History	5.5%
Nutrition Sciences	5.4%
Pharmacy	5.3%
Information Systems and Management	5.3%
Foreign Language	5.2%
Interdiciplinary Studies	5.1%

Source: Duffin, E., "Unemployment rate of U.S. college graduates January 2019, by major." www. statisa.com.

Every person in the retail field, including myself, dreamed of going to New York after graduation. But for those of us who did get a chance to move to the Big Apple, most likely we could only secure a position paying $30,000 a year, with 50% of that being taken out for taxes and the other 50% going to rent.

With my first job, I made 60% more than that a year and would earn a raise after six months. Not to mention, the cost of living in Seattle was significantly less than New York. So, hell yeah my ass was going to Seattle whether I liked it or not. My one-way ticket was booked and my last suitcase was zipped up. My parents graciously went with me across the country to help me move. They also graciously told me that I was now cut off. In other words, I was financially independent.

In other words, "Make sure you packed all yo shit 'cause we're turning your room into a gym," "Don't ask us for anything 'cause you grown now," and "Make sure you start saving 'cause we want a five-star retirement home in 40 years with a jacuzzi and in-house masseuse." My father even tried to back collect on six months of my phone bill.

Was this a joke? No, this was chained freedom. It was no longer about whether your parents allowed you to do something or gave you money. I now had to say, "Hold on let me check my bank account!" before agreeing to attend any type of event or just go shopping with a friend. And to add on to your already existing financial hardship, most of you will be hit with your first student loan payment just six months after graduation.

Not six months after you've secured a job—six months after you've graduated, whether you have a job or not. I received my first bill for $441.27. That's like paying rent in Florida on top of the rent I was already paying in Seattle. I thought, "Where are they getting this $441.27 monthly payment from?" After just two months, I dialed the 1-800 number and had my payments cut in half. It was a bittersweet win. I knew I'd be in debt that much longer but at least I wouldn't be eating ramen and grilled cheese sandwiches for the rest of my life. As I show in the next figure, it's so important to know how to make a real-world budget—and stick to it!

FIGURE 3

MAKING A REAL WORLD BUDGET

Identify Your Fixed Expenses	Rent Utility Bills Insurance Loans
Develop a Savings Strategy	401K/403B Contributions Savings Account Contribution (10-20%)
Identify Your Variable Expenses	Groceries Transportation Personal Care + Toiletries Daycare

Luckily, I received a promotion, a $5,000 raise, and bonus eligibility around the same time my payments began. I completed my training program and was finally at the Assistant Buyer level in Nordstrom's shoe buying office. Amanda, one of the great mentors I had met at Nordstrom took me under her wing and kept me on her division's team. When my parents helped me move to Seattle, they had reached out to Mike, an old friend from their days at Cornell University. Mike just so happened to be a good friend of Amanda and arranged for us to meet as soon as he discovered I worked at Nordstrom. No connection is too far fetched, my friends. My parents hadn't seen Mike in over 20 years. To be honest, I had never even met him or even heard about him until I moved to Seattle. You never know who knows someone or is willing to help introduce you.

STARTING A NEW JOB

After my first week in the new role, I realized, "Oh shit, this is a big job!" I was a 21-year-old who was co-managing inventory, profitability, and vendor relationships for a $300 million business. I had no idea what I was doing, but my mentor believed in me, so I knew I had to step up to the plate. I was on a team with three veteran assistants, all of whom were 7-15 years older than me. One of the assistants, Brittany, could not stand the amount of questions I asked her on a daily basis. She did not try to hide her annoyance with me. I was frustrated. I couldn't do anything without asking for help because I had never done most of these tasks before.

During my first month, Brittany pulled me aside to a conference room. She told me that I was asking too many questions and that I needed to start figuring things out on my own. I went home and cried. I was so used to always being the best at everything. I couldn't deal with the feeling of not knowing what I was doing. Like many new graduates, I wanted to be perfect at my job instantly.

It wasn't until I made my first big mistake that I realized it was a normal feeling to be uncomfortable in a new role. While my boss and her counterpart were in New York meeting with vendors, me and the rest of the assistants stayed back in Seattle. All of the assistants had a lot on their plates.

Since I was still transitioning, I didn't have much to do. Brittany decided to hand over one of her projects to me. She needed me to write an order in our system for 300 pairs of black pumps for a customer at one particular store. The customer needed the shoes for members of her choir. She handed me two pieces of paper stacked together. The paper on the top had the total shoe availability while the paper on the bottom had the actual number of pairs she needed me to order. Without knowing, there was a second piece of paper on the bottom, I began entering the order into the system. As I entered the order, I thought to myself, "Wow, this is a really big church group." In my gut it didn't feel right, but I didn't want to ask Brittany any questions. I submitted the order anyway.

A couple days later Brittany receives an email that 3,000 pairs of black pumps had arrived in our warehouse. She immediately looks at me and says, "How many pairs of pumps did you order for the church group? I calmly said, "I ordered everything that was on the sheet you gave me." She began panicking. It turns out I ordered all 3,000 pairs from the total availability versus the 300 pairs listed on the second piece of paper she intended me to order. At this point I'm on the verge of tears. This was a $300,000 mistake. I knew I was a goner. I felt so dumb for making such a big mistake. Luckily, the vendor agreed to take back the additional 2,730 pairs we ordered and we received all of our money back. My boss returned from New York and chuckled when I told her what happened. I expected a scolding at the very least, but she brushed it off.

There will always be people who will try to thwart your success. Let's refer to them as Brittany, or Brian, if it's a male.

TYPICAL TRAITS OF A BRITTANY OR BRIAN

- **These People Are Not Team Players.** They want all of the credit in order to make themselves look good. If their work is finished and they see others drowning in their workload, they typically will not offer to help.

- **They're Jealous.** This jealousy stems from insecurities. Brittany or Brian feels threatened by you.

- **They're Conniving**. Brittany or Brian wants others to share the same feelings towards you. An example could be inviting other teammates to lunch and purposefully excluding you.

- **They're Strategic.** If your Brittany or Brian is smart, he or she will not treat you poorly or differently around people who matter (e.g., your immediate supervisor or boss).

DEALING WITH YOUR BRITTANY OR BRIAN

- **Be the Bigger Person.** Don't pick up Brittany or Brian's bad behaviors. Continue to treat her or him with respect while still sticking up for yourself.

- **Stay true to you.** If you have an opinion, share it. Don't let Brittany or Brian's attitude derail you from excelling.

- **Help Others Even More Than You Primarily Would.** Be an example for others. You know how it feels to deal with a Brittany or Brian. You don't want others dealing with the same thing. A good leader inspires others around them.

- **Get Help as Needed.** If Brittany or Brian's behavior persists longer than you are comfortable or can deal with, you need to talk to someone, primarily your boss, and provide them with documented examples. These examples will build and support your case.

At the end of the day, I worked for my boss. Brittany and I were on the same organizational level. My boss and I were on the same page, and she understood there was going to be a learning curve. Brittany had momentarily affected my confidence in my competency to fulfill my job responsibilities. I never let that happen again. I deserved to be there just as much as she did. After about five months, I finally felt comfortable in my role. Brittany and the two other assistants had been promoted and I was now the veteran assistant. I was given additional responsibility, took on projects on my own, and presented them to leadership. Brittany had even reached out to me and asked for help on a few things after her promotion.

And yes, I did help her—with a smile.

LIFE LESSONS
DURING MY FIRST JOB

Here are some valuable lessons that I learned during my first job:

- **Create a Budget.** Make a budget and stick to it.

- **Find a Mentor.** Having at least one person in leadership who really supports, believes in you, and provides you with professional insight can do wonders for your career. It is just as important for you to maintain this relationship, as it is to do your own job responsibilities.

- **Give Yourself Time.** It's normal to feel uncomfortable in a new role—perfect takes time and practice.

- **Keep calm.** You are a human being and you are allowed to make mistakes.

- **Be Open to Learning.** After identifying a mistake, be apologetic and solution oriented. After owning up to your mistake, how can you solve the problem? How can you ensure this won't happen again in the future?

- **Always Trust Your Gut.** You're smarter than you give yourself credit for. If I had just asked questions, I would have never submitted an order for 3,000 pairs of shoes.

- **Don't Disclose Your Age in the Workplace.** As a young person, coworkers think it's OK to ask you this question. Frankly, it's unprofessional. You don't see me asking the lady on the fourth floor with dark circles and wrinkly hands how old she is. Many of my peers automatically associated my age with immaturity without even getting to know me. They treated me differently because of it. If someone asks you this question, simply respond with, "I'm not comfortable answering this question" or if you're as sassy as myself, "Old enough to work here" suffices as well.

CHAPTER TWO

Setbacks and Promotions: The Corporate Political Whirlwind

Everything seemed to be going right in my life. I still wasn't in love with Seattle, but I was content with my weekend outings for drinks, brunch, and outdoor activities with friends.

Eleven months after my promotion, Nordstrom announced we were going through an organizational restructure. After only being in the workforce for a little over a year, I had no idea what this meant. It turns out the company was eliminating more roles than it was creating. A few people would be promoted and many would be demoted. I learned quickly that this had nothing to do with an individual's skill set or performance, yet had everything to do with corporate politics and strategic placements.

I immediately became nervous. At that point, I had a great reputation but knew that as a recent grad, I had significantly less experience than the veterans around me who had worked their way up from the sales floor for years.

During our informational meeting, Lauren, our divisional vice-president, informed my team about a change in the merchant training program. Merchant-in-training grads would no longer be promoted straight into assistant roles. They would be moved into analyst roles. This meant more grunt work, less strategy, and more execution. A part of me knew it made more sense. I personally felt like I had been thrown in the fire after completing my program, but after five uncomfortable months, I'd figured it out. The second thought that came to mind was, " Well, what the fuck is going to happen to someone like me who has been in an assistant role for almost a year?" I compared the reality of getting demoted to eating Spam after eating filet mignon for a year. It didn't make sense. I expressed my concerns to my manager and let her know I had no desire to be put in the newly created role nor did I have any desire to switch departments.

Word eventually reached my mentor, Amanda, and other members of the leadership team. They reached out to me, told me I was a valuable member of the team, and that a demotion would not happen. Their words immediately put me at ease. After all, my mentor was pretty high up on the totem pole and I knew she supported me.

Weeks went by and my division's leadership finally began to announce the new structure. I received an invite for a meeting on Wednesday at 4 p.m. Christina, my counterpart on the team, had mentioned she was approached about being in the lower level position and was pissed as hell. Christina was my girl. We got along extremely well and disclosed way more information to each other than we probably should have. Christina had come from the marketing department and was about eight years older than me. Leadership knew the buying office wasn't for Christina and deep down she knew it, too. When Christina told me this, I knew it was coming down to either her or myself being put in the new role. I then realized it was so much easier for leadership to justify demoting a recent college grad than someone who had been with the company for years and was unhappy in their role. Even though I had been assured a demotion would not happen, I was still uneasy.

NAVIGATING PROFESSIONAL SETBACKS

Two days prior, my six-year-old family dog, Ripley, was diagnosed with cancer, and we were told he had less than a year to live. I was devastated. I prayed that whatever they told me in that meeting would be good news because I knew I couldn't emotionally take any more bad news that week. I walked into their office and both members of leadership greeted me with a big smile. "Baylie, you are definitely a strong member of the team. We can tell this is natural for you, we see you having a long-term career with the company, and we know you are going very far. We've had to make really hard decisions with this reorganization and feel you can serve as a leader in the new role…"

I immediately froze. This was actually happening. I felt like I had been hugged and slapped in the face at the same time. I was being demoted. I couldn't believe it. I just looked at them as they continued to speak. To be honest, I don't even remember what else was said because I was so upset. I was finally asked, "How are you feeling about this?" I immediately broke down crying (unprofessional, I know). I apologized and told them it had been a really rough week for me. I was running on no sleep and had been crying myself to sleep after finding out the news about my dog. They both comforted me and even said I could go home to see him and my family for a few days. It really was nice of them. They could have said, "This is what's happening so take it or leave." I knew they cared about me professionally and personally. They had so many hard decisions to make and I couldn't help but only think about myself. There were more senior members of my team who had been in their roles for four years and were demoted to assistants. I walked back to my desk, grabbed my purse, and went home. I was emotionally drained. As I waited for the bus (yes, people who work downtown commute to work via bus in order to avoid $300 monthly parking), a guy who didn't look too sane, walks up to me and asks if he can try on my sunglasses. I coldly respond, " Not today" and walk on to the bus.

The first thing I did was head to Safeway. My cart consisted of chocolate brownies, pizza, and hard cider. I attempted to eat my feelings until I realized it wasn't helping. In between blowing my nose and drying my tears, I grabbed my computer and began aggressively applying for jobs in New York and California. Now that I wasn't going to be happy in my job, and we all know I wasn't happy in Seattle, it was time for me to go.

I was angry, embarrassed, and ashamed to say the least. I knew I was a stronger assistant than a few others in my department. I didn't understand why I was being directly affected by the reorganization. Not only was I being demoted, but I was being moved to a different department who did double the volume of my current one. And if that wasn't enough, I was asked to peer mentor, Courtney, who would also be moved to the department. I knew this was a test. My boss had put on my mid-year review that I needed to work on training others and mentoring. It's not that I didn't like Courtney as a person. She was extremely immature, and I had absolutely no patience for her or really anyone for that matter. She also came through the same program as me a year after I finished. It was interns like her who led to Nordstrom's decision to move us into analyst roles.

The following day, the company sent out an email with the new team structure. My inbox and instant messenger began to crowd from coworkers wanting to know what happened. I began to receive looks of sorrow from coworkers as I walked to the bathroom, down the hall, or to the lunchroom. I don't think anyone enjoys being looked at like a sad puppy dog. Many of those who knew my dislike for Seattle were scared this reorganization would cause me to leave the company and Seattle altogether. Boy, were they right.

I decided that night that I wanted to be in this new role for the least amount of time possible. I applied to every internal assistant buyer role available and every external role posting I saw. If I received a promotion at Nordstrom before an external job offer,

I would stay till the end of March in order to collect my year-end bonus and use the money to relocate. I had one week before starting the new role and I started getting reckless to where I no longer gave a flying fuck. I was reaching out to contacts and applying to external postings at work. I let my emotions get the best of me. I was bitter. Someone at work could have easily seen me applying, or worse, one of our external partners could have told someone on our leadership team.

THE ROAD TO A PROMOTION

A week later, Courtney, myself, and the rest of the company began our new roles. I reported to the buy planner, Dave. Dave was in his early 30s and had two full arm sleeves of tattoos. He had a great reputation and I was excited to work for him. I just wasn't excited about the circumstances. He knew how tough the reorganization had been on me and had been extremely understanding.

After about two weeks in the role, I felt extremely discouraged. I wasn't being challenged. The job was simply right clicking throughout the day and filling out forms. I missed the analytical and strategic piece of my job. To top it all off, I hadn't heard back from any of the many external jobs I applied to. I was miserable. I decided to touch base with my manager and sent him a meeting request for the following day.

I began the conversation with "Dave, I'm not being stimulated... at all. Though I want to be in this role the least amount of time as possible, I feel that I can contribute so much more to the department and need to be given more responsibility. If that means I need to stay later in order to do so I'm fine with that." I think he appreciated how honest I was. He was completely receptive and mentioned working with Kristina on a new project. Kristina was a more senior assistant buy planner who was extremely smart. I knew I could learn a lot from her and was grateful to have the opportunity.

Two weeks later, I began to interview internally for other assistant buyer and buy planner roles in other divisions at my company. I made sure leadership had given me their blessing. In this world, there was no getting a promotion unless leadership approved, whether you were qualified or not. For the first time in weeks, I was excited. This would be my opportunity to ask for a raise, work with a new team, and get experience in a different division. Interviews made me somewhat nervous but to be honest, I was always an extremely well prepared interviewee.

PREPARING FOR YOUR INTERVIEWS

An interviewer will take many things into consideration. I've highlighted a few important points below:

1. **Presentation:** How do you present yourself? How do you put yourself together? If you look like you just rolled out of bed, you're probably not going to get the job. Is your shirt wrinkle free? Did you shower? Do you smell OK? Luckily, this has always been a category that works in my favor. Interviewers look at me and see a poised and well-dressed

African American woman working in a predominantly White field. Since companies like to pride themselves in being diverse, I was a shoo-in for any company. I'm not saying this was the only reason I got some of the jobs in my career. However, I am saying that my presentation has helped tremendously in my career.

2. **Qualifications:** Qualifications are important, however, if you don't look the part, none of these things will matter. The interviewer can read your resume and see that you've taken an accounting class or worked for a start-up company. However, it's your job to be able to verbalize how you will use these skills in the role to ultimately benefit the company.

I took a Business Communication class my last semester of college and it was probably one of the most beneficial classes I could have taken my entire college career. Mrs. Cooper explained the importance of a verbal professional summary and had each person practice in front of the class.

This summary should be less than 90 seconds and should give the interviewer an overview of your previous experience without having to look at your resume. I not only mastered reciting my professional summary, I also mastered the delivery. While delivering, I always had a passionate, exciting tone in my voice. I wanted the interviewer to know I was passionate and confident in my career path and could this bring the same passion and excitement to the role I was interviewing for.

3. **Personality.** Personality is a contributing factor. How well do you and the hiring manager mesh? Hiring managers want to make sure you will get along with their managing style as well as the other personalities on the team. They pretty much want to make sure you're not an asshole and can get along with current members of the team. This was also a test I always passed with flying colors. I'm an extrovert. I've found that confidence helps tremendously in any interview. You have to remember that every interview, no matter the field, is an opportunity to sell yourself. Even if it's not the interviewer's direct question, find a way to answer the question while providing an applicable example of your exemplifying qualities and skills. You can get a better idea of how to have the best possible interview in the next figure.

FIGURE 4

TODAY'S INTERVIEW LANDSCAPE

80% of available jobs are **never** advertised

20% of applicants get an interview

50% of applications are weeded out

118 The average number of people who apply for any given jobs

40 minutes: The time for the average interview

After three interviews, I finally received a job offer in the accessories division for an assistant buy planner role with a 13% increase in salary—the exact amount I asked for. It was a proud moment for me. After a rollercoaster month and a half, I was finally getting the promotion I worked towards. And to top it all off, I had received a cumulative 25% increase in salary after being in the workforce for only 18 months. It was a blessing in disguise. I would not have received this raise without the organizational restructure happening.

I don't think anyone could have predicted what the next five months of my life would look like. I learned the following lessons from my professional setback:

LIFE LESSONS
FROM MY PROFESSIONAL SETBACK

- **You're at the Bottom of the Totem Pole.** As a recent grad, you're at the bottom of the totem pole, regardless of how well you've performed.

- **Get It In Writing.** Words aren't worth the paper they're written on—don't accept verbal promises, get it in writing.

- **Control Yourself.** Don't allow your emotions to get the best of you.

- **Don't Burn Bridges Within a Company.** You never know when you are going to need the goodwill of leadership.

- **Be Honest With Your Manager.** If you're feeling unfulfilled in your position, try to provide proactive ways to improve both your situation and the company.

- **Save The Shit Talking For Outside The Workplace.** Don't let work instant message get you in trouble.

CHAPTER THREE

Navigating Your Personal Life Within The Life of Your Career

According to an article from "Sales Force," 44% of millennials say, if given the choice, they would like to leave their current employers within two years. "A perceived lack of leadership-skill development and feelings of being overlooked are compounded by larger issues around work-life balance, the desire for flexibility, and a conflict of value."[1]

When you already don't love your job and are working an excessive number of hours so that you can't even enjoy your personal life, you're on a downward spiral. My first day on the new job, I realized how different this division's operation was from my old department. How could processes at the same company be so different? My previous team valued continuous improvement and the importance of doing things efficiently versus working long hours. After a week on the job, I noticed how more advanced I was than the other assistant buy planner on the team.

1. Sales Force. https://www.salesforce.com/blog/2017/02/streamline-remote-working-team.html. Accessed April 22,2017

Don't get me wrong. I loved working with Cassandra. She was a team player, very welcoming, and was open to many of my suggestions on how to do things more efficiently. But it was clear she'd never been given the chance to make decisions on her own and drive results.

We reported to the same manager, Julie. It was immediately apparent that Julie was way more hands on than I was used to. She needed to approve everything before I could make a decision. She also liked being cc'd on 80% of the emails I sent to our external partners. I would often receive an email from her after anything I sent with a correction on how she would have worded the email with a reminder to do something I already knew I needed to do. I thought to myself a few times: "Does she think I'm an idiot?" The micromanaging expressed her insecurity and wasn't a reflection on me. There have definitely been instances I've asked a mentor or boss to proofread something, but for a basic response to a vendor about something not pressing, I'm pretty sure I am able to handle that on my own.

Julie loved to work at home after hours, especially on weekends. Every Monday I would come into the office to 15 emails she had sent me with suggestions and more to-dos, many of them for things I had already completed. My department had gone through a significant amount of turnover before my arrival and I found myself spending my time putting out fires. It was draining to say the least. I hate apologizing to begin with so having to apologize to vendors and members of my leadership team for the mistakes of others killed me. It was a bad look.

One day most of the team happened to be on paid time off. Stephanie and I were the only ones in the office from the team. Stephanie had joined the team the same week I did, so we were in the same "I'm so tired of putting out ya'lls damn fires" boat.

Dorian, my boss's boss, was aware of one of the fires and called Stephanie and me to his office. He asked why these things had been missed and not completed earlier. Stephanie was a lot softer spoken than me, so naturally I knew I needed to be the one to answer his question. It took everything in me not to say, "Dorian, this team is a hot-ass mess and so many things were not done before our arrival. We do not have a handle on the business and barely have enough time to analyze performance, let alone react."

Instead, I swallowed my anger and responded with one of the most grown-up things I've ever said, "Dorian, you're absolutely right. Stephanie and I don't manage this brand. However, with most of the team out of the office right now, we'll dedicate our day to correcting the problem and will report back to you by the end of the day with an update and our action plan for things not completed."

Stephanie didn't say a word. Both of us were dealing with huge amounts of anxiety from joining the team. This was one of many times I had to go into Dorian's office with my tail between my legs for mistakes others had made. I had to learn how to push aside pride.

I grabbed coffee with my mentor and explained the situation. I wanted to beg her to take me back, but of course I couldn't do that. I decided I just needed to stick it out.

My work days were long. I was getting to the office around 8 a.m. and leaving at 8 p.m. There were even days I was at the office till 10:30 p.m. I'm a hard worker and totally get that there are times in my industry that require additional devotion. However, I was not willing to spend every night at the office. On top of that, my boss said we needed to start working on weekends in order to catch up.

 Two months into my promotion, I received an email from a company I'd contacted during my Apply-to-every-job-not-in-Seattle binge. The job was for an inventory planner in San Francisco. I passed the HR screening and was scheduled to have three phone interviews with members of the team. I was so ready. I had recently fallen in love with San Francisco on a personal trip and was thrilled about the possibility of moving there. I began apartment hunting online. I thought, "Let me think this into reality."

A week later, the company decided they wanted to fly me out to San Francisco to interview in person. My outgoing flight was at 8 a.m. and I would fly back to Seattle that same day at 4:30 p.m. I woke up around 5 a.m. and drove myself to the airport. I texted my boss around 7:00 a.m., telling her I was sick and couldn't come in that day. I knew this was a lie and I felt bad about it.

If you find yourself in a similar situation as me, other ways you could interview without telling your boss exactly what you are doing is simply saying, "I need to take a personal day." You do not need to give details. You do not need to come up with some elaborate story. I know some people who just tell their boss that they are interviewing and I'd personally advise against this. Your boss is your boss, not your friend. At the end of the day, they have their best interest at heart, not yours. You do not want them knowing you are a flight risk.

HANDLING FAMILY EMERGENCIES

I had three back-to-back interviews. Each one went better than the one before. I figured there was no way they weren't going to hire me. A week went by and I heard no update. I began to get nervous. Had I been overly confident? Another week passed and they still hadn't made a decision. I couldn't believe it. I legit killed that interview. A whole month passed, and they finally relayed to me that they decided to go with another candidate who had a little more experience. I was absolutely devastated— and not about the job. I was devastated because this meant I was stuck in Seattle even longer. This job was supposed to be my salvation. A month passed and I was even more miserable than before. I hated my job to a point where I would get anxiety as I got ready for work. Luckily my mom was in town for work gig. She's a corporate trainer and traveled globally 80% of the year delivering keynotes, motivational speeches, and performance coaching services.

I desperately needed some Mommy time. She was staying

at a hotel nearby. I made it very clear at work that I could not stay late. As soon as the clock hit 5 p.m., I ran out the door. I was so excited to see my mom that I speed walked to her hotel and banged on the door. She opened the door and I was immediately confused. She looked like she had been crying. Was she not excited to see me? "Mom, are you OK?" I asked.

"Sorry, I'm watching a sad movie." She continued to cry. Finally, I asked her what was really going on. She handed me the phone and said I needed to speak with my father because she couldn't tell me. I knew what was going on. It was Ripley, my dog. I held my breath as I waited for him to speak. "Ripley's not doing well," my dad said. "He's not eating and has been going to parts of the house by himself to be alone. I don't think he has much longer."

I knew this day was coming but had no idea it would be this soon. Ripley was like our child. He was the light of our family. When 20 things were going wrong, he was the one thing that was always right. Ripley was only six. Why was he being taken away from us so soon?

After hours of crying and sleeping, my mom and I decided we needed to leave the hotel and get something to eat. My mother had a weeklong work trip in Europe after her Seattle gig. She was praying Ripley could fight until she returned. I begged her to let me fly home to Houston to say goodbye.

A year after college graduation, my parents had relocated from

Orlando, Florida to Houston, Texas. It had been more than four months since I'd last seen Ripley and I couldn't fathom the idea of not getting to say goodbye. My mother booked me a flight for that Friday to return the following Monday night. I let my boss know the next day that I'd have to work from home on Monday, as I had a family emergency I needed to be present for.

I arrived in Houston and waited for my dad to pick me up. I had never been to Houston before. This obviously wasn't a vacation trip. I had no interest in seeing anyone or anything besides Ripley for the next three days.

I watched my dad pull up in front of me with the right back seat window down and a furry little white Maltipoo sticking his head out. Through his pain he still managed to greet me like he hadn't seen me in years. It was depressing to think this might be the last greeting I would ever receive from him. I cried in silence all the way home. I witnessed in person the pain Ripley had been going through. It broke my heart.

I spoiled him rotten that weekend. We played, cuddled, and slept together. He followed me from room to room. I slipped him a piece of jerk chicken and gave him his favorite snack, beef jerky.

Monday came around and I worked from home. Before I knew it, I was packing up and preparing myself for one of the saddest goodbyes I would ever have. I was so overwhelmed. Life was kicking my ass. I felt like I was drowning in a two-foot pool, knowing I could save myself, but not having the energy to. I lay on the floor and held him as tight as I could without hurting him. "I need you to fight, Ripley. You can't leave me."

I returned to Seattle. Ripley managed to hold on for three more weeks. My mom was back from her business trip. I spoke with my parents every day on his status. One Monday I didn't hear from them all day.

The next day, I received a text from my parents while at work, letting me know it was time and that I needed to say my goodbyes. I ran to a conference room and Face Timed my dad. Ripley was sprawled out on the garage floor. My mom was holding him and crying. I said my goodbyes, walked slowly back to my desk, grabbed my belongings, and left. I needed to get myself together. I had never experienced this painful feeling in my heart before. I know I sound like a privileged brat, but it's true. I've lost two grandparents but I wasn't close to either. Frankly, if you're not a dog owner you will never understand the type of loss a deceased pet will bring.

On Wednesday, I was too upset to get to the office and worked from home. As I worked between sobs, I received three instant messages from my boss. Work still needed to get done. My plan was to log off right at 5 p.m., but my boss sent me a message asking, "You're going to finish this and send it to our vendor tonight, right?" I finally logged off at 7 p.m. My face was swollen from crying and I'd run out of tissues. I needed food and my bed.

By Thursday, the swelling had gone down a little bit, but I still looked like shit. Of course I really didn't care. I get on the bus and it's packed as usual. I have no choice but to stand. Six minutes into the ride I begin to feel dizzy. My vision starts to blur and I feel my legs begin to give out. I'm about two seconds from passing out and finally ask someone if I can sit. Of course they immediately get up. Everyone in Seattle is so nice. If I were anywhere else they would have assumed I was hung over. I take a seat and lean over. I've never felt this sick in my life. I finally make it to work. The day was a blur, but I surprisingly made it through. After an hour-long conversation with my parents, they convince me that I need to go to the doctor about my dizzy spell. It was the third one I had gotten in three months and something was up. I make an appointment online for the next day.

Receiving A Critical Life Diagnosis

Friday was the DAY FROM HELL. Everything that could have gone wrong went wrong. My counterpart and I were drowning in unrealistic deadlines. I dreamt I could flash forward two weeks to my planned trip to Florida. I had my appointment scheduled for 1 p.m. and I had a scheduled meeting with my boss at noon. I let my boss know that I had a doctor's appointment and she immediately asked me if I could reschedule. NO! At the end of the day your health is most important.

She begins to tell me that the project Stephanie and I had been working on needed to be done that day. My eyes begin to bug out of my head. I said, "Julie, this is a three-day project at the very least. There is no way this can be complete today." She responds by saying, "I'll talk to Dorian, but I'm pretty sure he's going to say this needs to get done today as well."

I walk back to my desk grab my belongings and call an Uber to get to my doctor's appointment. I filled out the paperwork and head into her office. After explaining my symptoms of dizziness, insomnia, and irritability, she diagnoses me. "You are dealing with major anxiety from your job, your unhappiness in Seattle, and the death of your dog. I'm going to prescribe you something, but it sounds like you need to make a life change."

Well, no shit. She pretty much told me everything I already knew but didn't have the balls to do. She handed me a prescription for Xanax. I left the office in silence and headed back to work. My boss joined me at my desk to inform me that Dorian would like the project done that day. Of course, Dorian didn't know all that it would entail. I gave Julie the nastiest look I could come up with and turn around to face my computer. It took everything in me not to say, "Heifer, I told you this was impossible."

CONVICTED DECISION MAKING

Five o'clock hits and I see members of my team start to pack up. It's Friday, they should be, right? I'm still plugging away on this project and am probably only 15% complete. At 6:15, I finally realized that it would not be worth it to stay until midnight and still not be finished. I instant messaged my boss.

Me: *Hey, this is still not complete and I have to go.*

Julie: *OK.*

And that was that.

I walked out the door. Your personal life should always win. I met a friend for a drink and vented for hours. I lowered my voice once I realize Stephanie from my team had the same idea and was also venting with one of her friends four tables down. I check my phone and see that Julie had sent me a touch base meeting request first thing Monday morning. After having my initial touch base cancelled five times, I finally had my first one after being on the job for three months. As soon as I "start acting up," she puts one on my calendar immediately.

I called my parents on the way home and continued to vent. I told them, "There's no way I'm going to take Xanax because of a job." When your work life starts to affect you mentally, let alone physically, it's time to move on. No job should drive you to insanity.

"Then quit," my mom said. She said it so nonchalant like it was no big deal. "You've been saying how miserable you've been for months. Why don't you do something about it?"

She was right.

Ripley was a prime example of how life is too short. It's emotionally draining to be unhappy all the time. I hadn't really thought about quitting my job without finding another one. When the San Francisco job didn't work out, I was so determined to find another job that it hadn't crossed my mind that there was another way out. I had been applying to multiple jobs in New York and hadn't heard back from any of them. It's nearly impossible to get a job at my level in New York when you don't already live there. They can find someone who will do the same job for 50% of the pay and no relocation support.

I had once mentioned to my dad's sister that I wanted to move to New York. She always told me I had a place to stay. At this point it was already almost midnight but I called my aunt anyway. She was up. She knew how miserable I had been and had confirmed that I could stay with her until I got on my feet in New York.

After one of the worst weeks of my life, I had finally decided I was leaving Seattle for good. As soon as I said this out loud, it was like a weight lifted off my shoulders. I couldn't wait to turn in my two weeks notice. I started practicing out loud how I would turn in my notice. The next morning, I began working out the logistics of selling my car, shipping my belongings, getting out of my lease, oh and um...priority # 1: Getting a damn job.

Let thy hustle begin.

LIFE LESSONS
FROM SURVIVING A TOUGH BOSS

Here are some of the lessons I learned after having four different bosses in a matter of seven months:

- **Your Boss Has To Have Your Back.** Your boss needs to be your main support system. You need to feel that you and your boss have aligned goals. Does your boss see you in the VP level that you see yourself? Does your boss want to help you get there? This is extremely important especially for someone who is rather new in his or her career. We're at the bottom of the totem pole, my friends. You may not always have a voice in certain situations but it's reassuring to know your boss does. In this moment I needed my boss to have my back and express to her boss that this was an absolutely unachievable task.

- **Be Open To Your Boss' Feedback**. Your boss should give you positive and negative feedback on a daily basis. Nothing should be a surprise on your annual performance review. You should know the things you need to work on before this meeting. You should also know that feedback is not an attack against your character. It's a learning opportunity to help you grow, not to hinder your performance.

- **Your Personality Must Be Compatible With Your Boss.**
  Your personalities must mesh. I touched on this previously
  but wanted to give you some more examples when I say
  this. Does your boss's teaching style align with your own?
  Do you get along? Is your boss super organized and you
  work best with 50 Excel documents open at once and 600
  unread emails at a time?

Everyone is different, yet we all have to work together in
some shape or form. Save yourself the future hassle and ask
these questions during your interview. At this point in time, I
had been in the workplace for almost two years and already
knew I did not do well with micro management. Give me
direction, but give me free reign to think for myself and come
up with solutions, projects, and ideas on my own. That's what
you're paying me for, right? In every interview I stressed the
importance of my feeling valued in the workplace and feeling
that I had a voice.

For example, take my boss before Julie. He was a super laid
back kind of guy. We had similar interests in music and
after-work activities. He was a hands-off boss. He had a lot
on his plate, but what I liked about him was the fact that he
understood the importance of teaching. Since he was busy half
of the time, he paired me with a more senior level assistant in

order for me to get shoulder-to-shoulder time and learn from her. Every now and then he'd check in to see how I was doing. After a couple weeks, I told him I wanted more responsibility. That very day he handed me a new project.

CHAPTER FOUR

Operation: Get A New Job

I had my letter of resignation typed and ready to go. Over the
weekend I had conquered breaking the news to my roommate,
cancelling my monthly public transportation pass, emailing my
landlord, and making a dentist appointment for a new mouth
guard since I knew I would no longer have insurance. Now I just
needed to make it official and submit my notice.

When 10:00 a.m. rolled around, my boss tapped my shoulder and
asked if I was ready. I grabbed my notebook and stuck my letter
in between the front two pages of my planner. My boss, Julie,
started by saying, "Baylie, I know Friday was a little interesting
and I know everyone has a lot on their plates. I just want to get a
feeling for everything that's on your plate and how you thought
Friday went. I feel like something is going on with you."

You should always be able to articulate your feelings professionally. I don't think I could have handled that situation any better. In that moment, she needed to know I was upset. It was the only thing that woke her up. I was firm when I told her the task she was giving me was impossible and had an unrealistic deadline.

I responded, "I was told at 12 p.m. on Friday that a three-day project had to be done that day. When I told you on the spot how impossible it was, you brushed it off and still told me it needed to get done. I did not feel supported in that moment and I've been feeling like this hasn't been the right fit for me for awhile. I'd like to turn in my two-week notice, effective November 25.

Her mouth dropped. "I don't know what to say. What are you going to do?"

I told her I was moving to New York to be closer to family. She told me she understood about not liking where I was living and wanting a change.

She asked if I was still taking my vacation now that I was leaving and I said, "Sure am." Overall, my boss did handle it really well. I know she was just as overwhelmed as I was, but I had to do what was best for me. We hugged before leaving the conference room. I was proud of myself. I did what I said I was going to do.

My first step was changing my address on my resume so that
I now had a New York address. Now that I was moving to New
York on my own, companies needed to know that I did not
require relocation. Once I updated my address, I reapplied to
every single job I had ever applied to.

I had 18 days to find a job. Four of those days would be spent
in Florida for my college alumni reunion. I had initially blocked
out a week of vacation time and decided it would be in my best
interest to fly to New York directly from Florida to interview and
try and get my life together.

My second step was utilizing my connections. Once I turned in
my notice. I scheduled time to speak with each of my mentors
to tell them the news. I wanted them to hear it from me and
not someone else. However, the main reason was for them to
pass my resume along. I had built a great rapport with them
and I knew they had great connections in the industry. This is
why it was extremely important for me to leave the company
on good terms. Would it have felt good to tell my boss to fuck
off? Totally. But what good what it have done for me in the long
run? Don't ever burn bridges if you don't have to. This world is
smaller than you think.

My third step was to secure interviews. Many people don't
realize that you are in control of your job hunting process.
You can take the lead. After three days or so, five different
companies had reached out to me. After passing the recruiter's
initial phone screening, some companies wanted to meet me

immediately while others wanted to schedule additional phone interviews two weeks out. I took the opportunity to inform each employer that I would be in town for three days before my official move and would love to utilize that time to come in, meet the team, and learn more about the role. Not one interviewer objected.

Within four days I had secured five in-person interviews and one phone interview. I had a jam-packed trip, but I was more determined than ever to secure a job as soon as possible. I felt kind of embarrassed when people would ask, "Oh, you're moving to New York? What will you be doing?" My response would be "I'm still figuring that out." It's not like I'm going to tell a stranger I was two minutes away from having a mental breakdown due to a lethal mix of unhappiness and anxiety.

Looking back, I'm not sure why I was so self-conscious about my decision to move to New York without a job. No one understands what you're going through more than you do. I did this for me. I knew I had God's support (I had been constantly praying about this) and my parents' support. I did this to be happy. Clearly, my decision to leave had improved my attitude and mood tremendously so why did I care what people thought of my decision?

My boss' boss scheduled a sit-down with me the day of my flight to Florida. He had started in the division around the same time I did so we hadn't really built a strong relationship. I was curious as to what he would say in response to my sudden resignation. I walked in his office with my notebook in hand. As expected, he was surprised. He said, "Baylie, I wish you'd told me sooner. I could have done something or stepped in. Is there anything we can do to keep you? We haven't posted your job yet. We can forget about your notice."

There was nothing he could do or say. I had already made up my mind that I was leaving. This wasn't about money. I exited his office and quickly grabbed my suitcase to make my 2:30 p.m. flight. I was so close to freedom. I had to sprint to catch my damn flight.

LIFE LESSONS
FROM QUITTING MY FIRST JOB

Here are a few lessons learned after quitting my first job:

- **Don't Be Complacent In Misery.** Your personal life should always win. If you're not happy, do something about it.

- **Take Strategic Risks.** Knowing I wouldn't have an income when I moved to New York, I arranged to stay with my aunt rent-free. Always have a plan.

- **Stay Professional even in Unfortunate Situations.** Even though I was miserable, I still ended things on good terms. The world is too small and you never know who you'll work with later in life.

CHAPTER FIVE

Making Money Moves

N ow the road to happiness isn't happy and yellow with directions pointing "Go that way." If that were the case, we'd all be working at our dream companies in our dream jobs.

My travel itinerary was as follows:

- Thursday 1:00 a.m.: Land at Tallahassee Airport

- Sunday 2:00 p.m.: Drive to Orlando

- Monday 7:00 a.m: flight to JFK

- Wednesday: Flight back to Seattle (?)

At this point I still hadn't bought my flight back to Seattle. I wasn't really sure what I was waiting for. After a party-filled blur of a weekend in Tallahassee, I got in the car around 2:00 p.m. to head to Orlando. I was carpooling with a sorority sister and my parents were going to pick me up from her house. They happened to be in town for a gig. My mom was there for work, so I was staying in their hotel room for the night and would fly out the next morning to New York to start interviewing. I decided that I should probably buy my return flight at this point as well. Luckily I had a few miles I was able to use. I printed 15 copies of my resume at the hotel, knowing I would have no time once I got to New York.

The next morning I popped out of bed at 5:00 a.m. I was on a mission. Playtime was over. I landed at JFK around 9:30 a.m. and headed to my aunt's house in Queens. Her two cats greeted me at the door as I put my stuff down. I had my first phone interview at 11:00 a.m. with Fossil. I pulled out my resume and began to recite my elevator speech. I had become a pro at reciting and summarizing my experience in order to answer the "Tell me about yourself" question.

The phone interview was scheduled to end at 11:30 a.m. I then had to leave the apartment promptly at 11:45 a.m. to catch the subway to my 1:00 p.m. interview at Saks Fifth Avenue. Following my 1:00 p.m., I had 2:30 and 5:00 p.m. meetings set.

My 11:00 a.m. interviewer didn't call until 11:20 a.m. I felt a real connection with her and we both seemed to be hitting it off. Although the job was based in New York, my potential boss would be based in Dallas at Fossil's headquarters. I felt like this would give me the opportunity to really own my role and make decisions since she wouldn't physically be there all the time. I apologized at 11:50 a.m. for having to cut our conversation short. I knew I was cutting it close for my 1:00 p.m. interview. I grabbed my shoes and ran to the train.

I hustled and got to Saks Fifth Avenue's lobby at 1:05 p.m. I quickly signed in but then realized I had got on the wrong elevator. I had to go all the way up to then come all the way down to then go back up on a different side. I hadn't even had time to change into my heeled boots. I was wearing a professional business dress with socks and oxfords.

By the time I sat down with my interviewer, it was 1:12 p.m. I apologized and explained the elevator situation. I could tell she was not having it. After five minutes, her attitude shifted once she realized how qualified I was. I was working extremely hard to win her over. I offered real-life examples for every question she asked me.

Once I passed her test, she passed me off to her boss, the planning manager. I liked her a lot. I slyly dropped a hint that I was interviewing at a few other places so she knew that this was not a process I wanted to be dragged out. I wanted her to know that they were not the only place I was considering. I left the office feeling great. Even after being late, I knew they would offer me the job. I headed toward my next interview, looking for places to grab a bite to eat.

My next interviewer was with an actual agency that connected companies with prospects. They did most of the work for me with negotiating salary and setting up interview times. The caveat, however, was that you could not be recommended to a company if you had applied within a year. This was quite difficult for me because I had applied everywhere. I stayed open minded.

The recruiter loved me and seemed extremely passionate about finding the right fit for me. For those of you who have used staffing agencies for temp work, keep in mind that some companies are hesitant about hiring temps due to the amount of money they have to pay the agency to hire them as permanent—this can sometimes be extremely costly to the company.

The next day, I had another in-person interview with another agency I had been working with. I had a contact I had worked with when I almost moved to New York earlier in the year. The common question I was asked was, "What made you quit your job without another one?" It was a fair question.

Here's where professional discretion comes in. These employers did not need to know I was miserable in my new role and felt unsupported. I did not want them to view me as someone who bashed a company as soon as they left. Companies want loyal employees. In the next figure, I provide a list of best practices for having a great interview.

FIGURE 5

INTERVIEW
BEST PRACTICES

- [ ] Show up early and on time

- [ ] Dress appropriately

- [ ] Get mentally prepared

- [ ] Make friends with the receptionist

- [ ] Do your research and show up prepared

- [ ] Send a thank-you email to each person you interview with

So here's what I shared. I said, "I was at Nordstrom for over two years and although I loved the company and the culture, Seattle was not somewhere I saw myself being long-term. I'm originally from the East Coast and want to be closer to family. I want to love my personal life just as much as I love my career."

No one could argue with that. It was the truth. Yes, the end of my time at Nordstrom was far from ideal. However, it didn't change the fact that I had great experiences up to that point and had met so many amazing people. I left and headed back to my aunt's house. I had the rest of the day to start researching storage places, shipping costs, and apply to additional job opportunities.

Wednesday rolled around and I had a jam-packed day ahead of me. I had two interviews at two major company showrooms and then had to rush back to Queens to grab my suitcase and head to the airport for a 2:00 p.m. flight back to Seattle.

9:00 a.m.: I arrived right on time for the interview and met with Fossil's senior account executive. I loved her off the bat. She was so down to Earth and personable. She had great things to say about the team and structure. I had the phone interview with my boss who lived in Dallas. Two days after seeing the office in person, I was set on the company. Unfortunately, all of the leadership team was out of office and they were set on me meeting with the VP before any decision was made. I wouldn't be back in New York until I officially moved there 10 days later.

10:30 a.m.: The next interview was walking distance from the first and I arrived with 10 minutes to spare. Kate Spade's office was legit. Kate Spade had a major presence at Nordstrom and I was super excited to learn more about the role. The only downside was that it was for a wholesale planner role versus an account executive role. This would mean that my role would mostly be with numbers versus a combination of numbers, people, product, and merchandising.

I had searched the interviewer via LinkedIn and it was nice to see my role report to a Hispanic woman. In my industry there aren't many women of color. The hiring manager and I sat down in a conference room. They began with the typical interview questions. It was clear, however, that their chemistry was off. To be honest, it was super awkward. It seemed that the hiring manager felt the HR woman was taking over the interview and overstepping her boundaries.

Overall the interview went well, but I couldn't get past what I had just witnessed. It was a bad sign. What was the company culture really like? I speed walked to the train and hopped on the subway. I had a missed call and voicemail from Saks Fifth Avenue. They were calling to offer me the job. I couldn't believe it. Fuck, I actually did it! I was ecstatic until I heard the dollar amount they were offering me. It wasn't even 1% more than what I was currently making. After everything I had been through after college, I did realize that money wasn't everything. However, I wasn't trying to move to New York and financially struggle. New York's cost of living was roughly 60% more than Seattle.

I was grateful that God had opened this door for me. However, I wasn't sure if it was the right door. I told the recruiter that I was excited about the opportunity but was expecting a higher bump in salary and wanted to negotiate. I also reminded her that I was still interviewing for other roles and wanted to see where those led. She of course gave her spiel about all the other great benefits there were, but when it was clear to her how firm I was in an increased offer she said she would get back to me.

I called an Uber and headed out the door. I arrived at JFK, checked my luggage, and took a seat at my gate. "Baylie Robinson, it's about to be a busy 10 days," I thought. I had booked my one-way ticket back to New York for the Saturday after Thanksgiving. There was no turning back.

I walked back in the office after being gone a week. I had a few more meetings with old bosses and mentors set up. The next few days I tried to get as much work done as I could. I left at 5 p.m. every day because I knew I had a lot to do at home. My dad helped me post my car on Craigslist while I posted all my furniture online. When I moved to Seattle, we bought cheap furniture so I was not attached to any of it. I knew I would need to sell half of my belongings as I would not have much space once moving into a New York apartment.

Three days after receiving my first New York job offer and eight days before my official move date, the HR recruiter called me back with an updated offer. "They are increasing the offer by $2,000," she told me. Still disappointed, I thanked her and asked when they need a final decision from me. Her response was, "Tomorrow."

I began to panic. I loved the team at Fossil so much more than the team at Saks Fifth Avenue. I also heard many things about the company culture at Saks Fifth Avenue and wasn't sure if it was the right fit for me. On the other hand, I thought, "I am unemployed, how could I even think about turning down an opportunity when I have no job?"

My parents advised me to accept and then renege once I received another offer. However, I felt weary about doing that. I reached out to Fossil and let them know I had a job offer from Saks Fifth Avenue. The HR woman called me right away.

> **HR:** *Hi, Baylie. Thanks for letting us know. Can you let me know the compensation the other company offered? I answered her question.*
>
> **Me:** *Is there any way I can have a phone interview with the VP instead of an in-person interview? I loved speaking with everyone and I am most passionate about this position. However, I'm not sure I can turn down a concrete opportunity without having another one set.*
>
> **HR:** *I understand, Baylie. I will speak with the team to see if we can speed up the process for you. While I have you on the phone, can you please reconfirm the type of compensation you are looking for?*
>
> **Me:** *I am looking for an opportunity that pays X a year in order to cover the increase in cost of living.*
>
> **HR:** *That is typically more than what we pay associate account executives, but I'll see what I can do. I will email you by end of day if we are able to schedule a phone interview tomorrow with the VP.*
>
> **Me:** *Thanks so much. I really appreciate it.*

I called one of my mentors from Nordstrom, Cassandra, who used to work as an executive vice president. I explained my dilemma and told her the advice my parents had given me. She agreed with me that accepting the job and then turning it down was a bad idea. Our industry was too small and it was a bad look. She told me to have faith and pray about it. If it didn't feel right now, it wouldn't feel right later.

While on the phone, the HR woman sent me an email confirming a phone interview with the VP the next day at 10:00 a.m. EST which was 7:00 a.m. my time.

I woke up at 6:00 a.m. my time in order to give myself an hour to lose my "I just woke up and sound like a man voice" and eat breakfast. The VP called me promptly at 10:00 a.m. EST. It definitely wasn't as easy as I thought it would be. One minute she'd ask me questions on how to develop sales and budget plans and the next she'd ask what my favorite TV show was. I had no idea how I did.

The HR woman called me an hour later to let me know that the VP liked me a lot but still wanted to meet in person once I got to New York after Thanksgiving. I was not thrilled by the news, but I knew then what I had to do.

I had to turn down the offer from Saks. I slid into a conference room and made the call. Who in their right mind would turn down a job without having another? Me. The same girl who quit her job without having another one.

Six days before my official move date, Esteffania, a sorority sister of mine stayed for the weekend. I gave her a heads up that I was on a tight schedule, packing, and getting situated. I would

try to entertain her as much as I could. She had never
been to Seattle.

A man named Muhammad had reached out to me about
purchasing my car. Aside from finding another job, my biggest
concern was selling my car before moving because I clearly
couldn't bring it with me. I had no idea what I was going to do
if he didn't buy it. I was grateful Esteffania was there with me
that weekend.

Meeting someone off Craigslist as a single woman made me
so nervous. We met in a grocery store parking lot two minutes
from my house. He had been communicating with my father
to arrange to meet up and was surprised to see me get out the
car to greet him. I immediately requested his license and took a
picture of it to send it to my dad. I do not play with my life. Once
he inspected the car, I asked him if he wants to test drive it. He
said he has no insurance in which case, I needed to drive.

Esteffania hopped in the backseat while Muhammad got in
the passenger seat. After the test drive, Muhammad decided
he wants to purchase my car. We drove to the DMV in order to
put the car in Muhammad's name. Before getting out of the
car I requested for Muhammad to pay before our going in. My
dad listed the car at $5,000—a great deal and non-negotiable.
Muhammad clearly knew this before arriving, but he still
attempted to try my life. He said, "I can only offer you $4,500"
as he handed me a wad of bills. Clearly, Muhammad picked
the wrong 22-year-old female to try and get over on. "This car

is listed at $5,000. Take it or leave it. If you cannot offer $5,000, I can drive you back to the grocery store now."

He reached in his pocket and grabs the other $500.

That's what I thought Muhammad.

After transferring the car into his name, I stopped at my bank to deposit the money to make sure he did not pay me in fake bills. We then headed back to the grocery store to part ways. It was a bittersweet goodbye with the car, not Muhammad.

Shortly after, I was able to sell my entire furniture set, couches, and table. Anything I couldn't sell, I donated to Goodwill and wrote off everything on my taxes.

Four days before my official moving date I was barely packed. I was relying on friends and my current roommate to drive me places, whether picking up boxes or dropping me off somewhere. It was my last day of work and I couldn't believe my journey had come to an end. I left a handwritten thank-you note on each of my teammate's desks and left. I was officially free!

Three days before my official moving date was Thanksgiving. All of my friends were out of town except one. We grabbed an early lunch (the only last-minute reservation we could get) and spent the rest of the day packing, drinking, and listening to music at my house.

Two days before my official moving date, my mom arrived in town. She had a 24-hour layover in Seattle before going to Asia for work and rented a car so that I could have a mode of transportation. Little did she know, I needed her help to finish packing. My mom laughed as she walked through the door. "You do not look like someone who is moving across country in two days." She was right. It was a hot mess. I was overwhelmed with everything I had to get done and she was annoyed that I was about to put her to work two days before her major work assignment. Gotta love that woman for helping me!

On the day before my official move, I dropped my mom off at the airport in the morning and drove back home to continue packing my suitcases. The shipping company had picked up all my boxes the night before, so all I needed to pack were my valuables and clothes for the next few weeks. I dropped the rental car off and headed into the airport. Of course my luggage is over by six pounds and the flight agent didn't have a lenient bone in her body. People stared at me as I got on my hands and knees at the airport to begin swapping items into my carry-on and layering clothes onto my body. If only I had a dollar every time I've had to do this.

I opened my eyes at 9:00 a.m. as we landed on the runway. I was officially a New Yorker. My final interview at Fossil was the next morning and I was banking everything on it. I got my nails done, picked out my outfit, printed out additional resumes, and screenshot directions the night before.

The next morning I walk into Fossil's showroom and meet three different people: One VP from another division, a sales manager, and the VP I spoke with over the phone a few days before. I loved every person I met with. I left the interview feeling extremely confident. I emailed the VP I'd be working for and let her know that I felt it would be a really great fit for me. She responded the next morning.

> *Hi Baylie,*
>
> *It was great to finally meet you.*
>
> *We feel it will be a great fit as well.*
>
> *Hope to talk to you soon.*
>
> *Gina*

The next hour I get a call from Tiffani, the woman from HR. "We'd like to offer you the job with a compensation of X and the following benefits . . ."

They were paying me exactly what I asked for which was 10% more than my offer from Saks Fifth Avenue. As soon as we got off the phone, I cried. I had gone through so much in the last few months and I had finally done it!

In five months I had been demoted, flown to San Francisco and been turned down, promoted, lost my dog, been prescribed Xanax, quit my job, and moved to New York.

I secured a job two days after moving across country!

LIFE LESSONS
FOR MAKING LARGE LIFE TRANSITIONS

The following life lessons I learned in those five months sound quite simple but are so hard to do:

· **Always have faith.**

· **Follow your heart.**

· **Go after what you want in life.**

CHAPTER SIX

Life Will Never Be Fair

It was the beginning of a new journey—or so I thought. I was a few weeks into the role and had the benefit of being trained via phone for a week by my predecessor, Roxanne. Based on her interactions with Sylvia, my new boss, I could tell something was off with their relationship. I wondered why the girl before me was leaving. I became buddies with Kaitlin, the sales assistant on the team who had been working at Fossil for five months at that time and got the scoop. Apparently, Roxanne and Sylvia did not get along, but Kaitlin didn't tell me why. Looking back, I actually appreciated her discretion as it helped me form my own unbiased opinion.

For my first two weeks, Sylvia seemed cool but very hands on. I spent 80% of my days on the phone with Sylvia since she was based in Texas. I figured my time on the phone would decrease after I got more comfortable in my role. After my first two weeks, Sylvia was in town and wanted to grab dinner to get to know me better. I felt like we had really gotten somewhere. She told me that she was a straight shooter and that if anything ever bothered me to speak up. We spent the remainder of the week preparing for our Friday morning meeting so that we could enjoy our company holiday party on Thursday. This would be the first time I'd meet my client.

WORK PARTY ETIQUETTE

The party was an absolute shit show, but it was amazing. I only had two drinks since I had a big meeting the next morning, but my counterparts took full advantage of the open bar. They were a fun bunch of girls who I could actually see myself hanging out with outside of work. However, if there's one thing I can teach you, it's to never get wasted at a work party no matter how cool you think your boss is. An open bar is a trap. I've had a slip up myself, but I have learned to leave if I feel myself getting close to the point of no return. Instead, sip on your two drinks and people watch. It's just as entertaining with little to no risk. I went home that night beyond happy. I had a great job with great people in my perfect city.

Or so I thought.

After two months in the new role, I came to the conclusion that my boss was a little crazy. The amount of calls and instant messages never decreased. I'd go to the bathroom and come back with an email or a missed call. I'd step out for coffee and receive a text message from my boss asking where I was. It was too much. I finally told her over the phone that it was hard to get projects done with the amount of calls I was receiving. She responded, "I just want to make sure you know what you're doing." I'd receive my own projects and have the opportunity to present to our leadership team. Sylvia would take over the presentation and I'd barely be able to get a word in. A few weeks went by and it still didn't get better with my boss. I wasn't sure what to do. I couldn't fathom being in another shitty work situation after just getting out of one.

I received an email from a recruiter at another company. They were looking to fill an account executive position and a VP at Nordstrom had passed my resume along. I decided to go through with the interviews. It was a small company with a start-up feel. They were established internationally, but the U.S. was a new market for them. It was a risk. Given the current situation I was in with my boss, I decided to go through with the interview process. Knowing how much of a helicopter manager my boss was, it was hard to step out to interview.

The French company was very accommodating and scheduled my interviews after 7:00 p.m. This was a red flag that I unfortunately missed. The entire office was still there each time I came in after 7:00 p.m. If I was looking for a work life balance, which I was, there was no way I was going to get it there. While interviewing with the president, I was told I was junior for the role, but they still wanted me to continue the process. I eventually made it to the final interview and met with the CEO of the company. During the interview, he asked how old I was and if he could take my picture. Here was yet another red flag. It is illegal for any employer to ask you how old you are. Do not ever answer this question if asked. Although taking a picture is not illegal, it's really creepy.

The next figure provides an overview of both illegal and legal questions that you may encounter during an interview process. Again, you DO NOT have to answer ANY questions on the illegal list of questions.

FIGURE 6

KNOW YOUR RIGHTS

The following questions are **ILLEGAL** during an interview

What year were you born?

When did you graduate?

When did you first start working?

Are you married?

Do you have children?

Are you a U.S. citizen?

What is your background?

Do you have a disability?

Have you ever filed a worker's compensation claim or suffered a workplace injury?

Are you pregnant?

The following questions are **LEGAL** during an interview

How long did you stay in your last role?

What is your expected salary?

Do you have a high school diploma?

What college degree do you have?

Are you eligible to work in the United States?

Do you have responsibilities that would make it difficult for you to come to work?

Do you have reliable transportation?

I attributed his behavior to the company just being foreign. A few days later, I received an offer. It would be a minor pay cut. In hindsight, I let the idea of working for a luxury company, frequent work travel to Paris, and my helicopter boss at Fossil blindside me into accepting the offer. This is one of the biggest mistakes I've ever made in my entire career. Never make a life-changing decision without doing your research. You could end up in an even worse situation than the one you left. Acknowledge the signs. Create a pros and cons list. Get advice from a mentor. Utilize resources to get a true sense of the company.

After resigning and completing my two weeks at Fossil, I began my nightmare position at the French company from hell. I lasted three weeks before being wrongfully terminated. Let me start from the beginning.

WEDNESDAY, MARCH 2ND

On my first day, I worked 9:00 a.m. to 8:00 p.m. I had a total of two hours of overview training this day.

THURSDAY, MARCH 3RD

I worked from 9:00 a.m. to 9:00 p.m. I had to fly to Paris the next day and was preparing as best as I could for my meetings.

FRIDAY, MARCH 4TH

I got to work at 9:00 a.m. and continued to prep for my meetings. I left for the airport with my boss at 3:00 p.m.

SATURDAY, MARCH 5TH

I landed in Paris at 10:00 a.m. local time. I checked into the hotel and grabbed food. I later worked from 6:00 p.m. to 8:00 p.m.

MONDAY, MARCH 7TH

I worked from 9:00 a.m. to 8:00 p.m. During this time, I had a few 30-minute meet and greets with members on the Paris team to learn about their responsibilities.

TUESDAY, MARCH 8TH

I worked from 9:00 a.m. to 8:00 p.m. I was also given an event-planning project. The event typically takes six to eight weeks to plan. However, I was given only two weeks. On this date, I vocalized that I had never planned this type of event before and needed guidance. The president set up time for me to sit with my predecessor while in Paris. However, with my predecessor being so busy, she only had 15 minutes to review the process with me versus the original two hours my president had intended.

WEDNESDAY, MARCH 9TH

I worked from 9:00 a.m. to 12:00 p.m. before flying back to the

U.S. I told my boss I felt uneasy about the event given the lack of training I received and the tight deadline. She agreed that the event was too big of a project to be given to someone one week into a new role. With her being only a week in her role as well, she did not feel comfortable bubbling my concerns up. This is the day I realized how much of a coward my boss was.

THURSDAY, MARCH 10TH

I returned to the New York office. I worked from 9:00 a.m. to 9:00 p.m.

FRIDAY, MARCH 11TH

The president put a meeting on my calendar to review my follow-up from my Paris meetings. With everything on my plate, I had yet to complete all the follow-up, but I at least wanted to present what I had completed thus far. I was then scolded by the president for not having everything completed. My boss said nothing in my defense. At this point, I had only been in the office for one day after my Paris work trip. I was told I needed to have my boss and the VP look over my material prior to flying to Seattle on Sunday.

SATURDAY, MARCH 12TH

I worked from 10:00 a.m. to 1:00 a.m. the next day. I finally complete my meeting preparation and send to my boss and the VP as instructed. I received no response.

SUNDAY, MARCH 13TH

I fly to Seattle for a client meeting on Monday morning.

MONDAY, MARCH 14TH

I worked from 7:00 a.m. to 7:00 p.m. After the client meetings, I ask the VP and my boss for feedback on the meeting. They both shortly stated it went well.

TUESDAY, MARCH 15TH

I'm back in the New York office and worked from 9:00 a.m. to 9:00 p.m. My boss is out of town for additional work travel during this time.

WEDNESDAY, MARCH 16TH

The president tells me I need to complete a project that night at 8:30 p.m. This is a project that would take at least four hours. I realize then that I would have to complete an all-nighter in order to get it finished. I finally get approval from my predecessor after she reviews at 5:00 a.m. I then send the document to the Paris team at 6:00 a.m. In total, I worked straight from 9:00 a.m. to 6:00 a.m. the following day.

THURSDAY, MARCH 17TH

I worked from 9:00 a.m. to 7:00 p.m. On this day, I'm informed that the file I sent to the Paris team had corrupted due to the large size of the file and that the information was invalid. At

5:00 p.m., the VP then emails me asking to review an additional project with the team and to come up with a plan regarding our sales targets. At this point in time, we were only three months away from the end of our fiscal year and only had 32% of our sales plan in. She was essentially asking me, someone who had never worked in wholesale sales before and was two weeks into the role, to come up with a strategy on how to make up a $3 million dollar sales deficit. I leave the office at 7:00 p.m. due to my best friend being in town to visit. I had the following day off and there was no possible way I'd be able to complete all of the tasks that were given to me.

MONDAY, MARCH 21ST

My ball of anxiety returns. I worked from 9:00 a.m. to 8:45 p.m. I spent the whole day preparing for our weekly sales meeting. The president puts a meeting on my calendar at 7:00 p.m. to touch base from 7:30-8:30 p.m. that night. After waiting for the meeting to start, I ask my boss at 7:45 p.m. if the meeting is still happening. She says no. I finally leave at 8:45 p.m. I get home and go straight to bed.

TUESDAY, MARCH 22ND

I see an email from the president sent at 8:50 p.m. the night prior asking to touch base at 8 a.m. the next day. By the time I check my email, it's 8:30 a.m. and I had missed the meeting. I arrive at the office at 9 a.m. and my boss looks at me like she's seen a ghost. "I think we're ready to meet with you now." I walk into a room of stares.

The president immediately tells me that I'm no longer needed and they are letting me go. She states that I had failed to successfully complete anything that had been asked of me. I tried to defend myself, but my boss said absolutely nothing.

I sat in shock.

I'm told I will be paid through Friday.

I thought to myself, "Great. You just poached me from a stable (still not enjoyable, but still) job environment and are letting me go after two weeks but hey, thanks so much for my extra three days of pay."

I had received a maximum of six hours of shoulder-to-shoulder training spread out across the three weeks. I was never informed prior to being let go that my overall performance was under par. During my time at the company, I expressed to my manager how I felt overwhelmed and was expected to know how to do things with no training. She agreed and stated, "I can't believe they would give you this huge project one week into the role with no training on how to do it and no time to get it done."

It was one of the most toxic environments I had ever been in. I was bitter and angry. I wanted to burn the place down. I felt like they tricked me into leaving my previous job. I was also disappointed in myself for putting myself in that situation.

I grabbed my belongings from my desk and left. I went home and immediately started reaching out to attorneys. I wanted to fuck them over as much as they had fucked me over. After a few calls to attorneys, I learned I had absolutely no case. New York was an at-will employment state unless stated otherwise in a contract. I had no idea what I was going to do. After moving into a new apartment and paying first month's rent, a broker fee, and a security deposit, I had let my credit card get out of control. How was I going to pay my $1,500 rent with no income?

I had been in New York for only four months and I was unemployed again. I was embarrassed and ashamed. None of my friends knew what was going on with me. I stopped answering calls. I wasn't eating. I declined all invites. Well, with the exception of one.

After two days of being unemployed, I decided to go out clubbing with a friend. I attempted to cope with alcohol that night, which never helps.

My one night out consisted of a $600 Mackage leather jacket being stolen, a $350 watch gone missing, me being carried out the club by a 350-pound Black female security guard, a tear-filled Uber ride that took double the time to get to our destination because I had to puke every four minutes, and a sub from the nearby deli.

My mom was kind enough to loan me money until I got back on my feet so that I could pay rent and buy groceries. I absolutely hated accepting money from her almost as much as I hated filing for unemployment. I always had the ignorant assumption that unemployment was for poor or lazy people, but I was wrong. There are so many people who are put into similar shitty situations as mine. It completely changed my perspective. Here I was, a normal person who had experience and was more than capable yet on unemployment benefits.

It took a full week for me to get out of my negative headspace. I was more determined than ever to find not only a job, but also the right job. I had to log each job I applied to and what my job status was after each week in order to consistently receive my unemployment check. When connecting with my unemployment benefits representative, I was asked if I wanted to wait an additional week to file because I would receive a bigger portion (roughly $100 a week more). I quickly answered, "No, I don't plan on being on this for long anyway."

It took three weeks.

These three weeks were an emotional whirlwind for me. Three weeks of unintentional weight loss. Three weeks of praying that I'd find a job. Three weeks of my friends asking where I had been and why I hadn't responded to their calls. Three weeks of my parents checking in every day. Three weeks of countless phone and in-person interviews, email chains, and LinkedIn messages.

Three weeks and I was back to work. I had received a job offer from Tory Burch as an associate account executive. I called the unemployment 1-800 number to report I had found a job. Before I hung up, the representative says to me, "Wow, you weren't on this long at all. Most people are on this for months, sometimes even years. Good job!"

I grinned from ear to ear. I said, "I guess I'm not like most people. Thanks."

LIFE LESSONS
FROM MY NIGHTMARE JOB FROM HELL

Looking back on this moment in time, here's what I would have done differently and the lessons I learned: LISTEN TO YOUR FUCKING GUT AND ACKNOWLEDGE THE RED FLAGS!

Don't ever let a sucky circumstance blind you into getting into an even suckier one. Here are a few red flags I saw but failed to act on:

- **Pay Attention to Office Hours and Culture.** My interviews were scheduled for 7:00 p.m. and later and everyone was still in the office. I noticed this and asked questions, such as "What's the work life balance? I received a very politician-like answer when I asked this, but the truth was right in front of me. 7:00 p.m. and later interviews and the entire office were still there ?!

- **Don't Reveal Your Age.** During my final interview with one of the executives, I was asked my age and if he could take a photo of me. It is illegal for an interviewer to ask your age. I knew this, but answered anyway. I figured his ignorance of U.S. laws could be attributed to the fact that he was foreign.

- **Do Your Research!** I did my research on Glassdoor and saw mostly negative reviews. I ignored them. After being let go, I connected with a contact that informed me a similar situation had happened to a fellow employee before me. She exclaimed, "I don't even think they know what they want."

PART TWO

Dealing with Others

CHAPTER SEVEN

Living with a Crazy Roommate from Hell

"Adulthood is the worst hood [I've] ever been to"

—Unknown

When I say crazy, I'm not referring to the dumb White girl I decided to sign a lease with. I'm referring to myself. After a handful of breakdowns, texting wars, and a visit from cops, I was so ready for my one-year lease to be over.

For those of you who are blessed enough to live alone after graduation, I envy you. The rest of us commoners have one or two roommates in order to cut costs or live in a centrally located area. Most college apartments have individual leases and roommate match services. In real life, this doesn't exist.

In general, there's one lease and one expectation: rent is paid on time. If your roommate can't pay rent on time, you're still responsible. During my first year in New York, I had my first nightmare of a roommate situation. After four weeks of commuting from Queens to Midtown Manhattan and exploring all boroughs of Manhattan each day after work and living out of two large suitcases half the size of the room I was staying in, I finally found a place to live in Nolita, a neighborhood close to SoHo.

Ashley and I met through a "roommate matcher." New York brokers liked to call themselves roommate matchers when in reality all they do is introduce you to someone else who has reached out to them and then it's up to you to decide if you want to live with that person. There's no questionnaire or anything. One guy persisted that I live with a girl who had a cat after I already told his ass I was extremely allergic. Ashley was at the same appointment viewing as myself with her boyfriend. They seemed young, but normal. She had just graduated and had a really great job in the city. Ashley and I took a risk and tried to lock down an apartment I fell in love with while both of us were out of town for the holidays. The broker was great and was able to FaceTime me while walking through the apartment. She was making more than me so I decided to let her get the bigger room for $200 more a month and I would take the smaller room in an effort to save money. She gave us explicit directions on all the steps we needed to take since we weren't physically there. The first step was mailing an official bank certified check for the one month's rent plus a deposit. I overnighted my certified check from Houston while Ashley mailed hers from Pittsburgh.

The next day I get a frantic call from the broker saying, "Ashley, mailed a regular check. Is this a joke? Are you guys serious about getting this apartment?" I immediately start to freak out. The company couldn't take the apartment off the market until they had the full deposit in their hands. If this girl caused me to lose the apartment and my money, we were going to have major problems. I call Ashley right away. She didn't answer. I texted her, "Hey, you were supposed to mail a bank certified check. We are going to lose the apartment if you don't send one ASAP."

She responds right away. I was thinking, "What the fuck were you doing two seconds ago when I called you?"

She replied, "OK. I will do that now."

There was no sorry or anything. This was the first of many red flags. Ashley didn't follow directions. We ended up securing the apartment and I showed up at the office to sign my paperwork. They couldn't give me the keys until Ashley signed, which would be a few days later. On move-in day I had to work a half day, so Ashley was given the keys. I asked her to text me when she got to the apartment so I could go straight from work.

10:00 a.m.: No text.

11:00 a.m.: Still no text.

12:00 p.m.: I call her. No answer.

1:00 p.m.: I call her a second time and she finally answers.

> **Me:** *Ashley, you were supposed to text me when you got to the apartment. I'm coming straight from work and have no way of getting in without the keys.*
>
> **Ashley:** *Oh, yeah sorry we're here.*

Well, no shit. They had been there for hours. Another red flag. I was so desperate to find a place in the city that I realized I did not do my due diligence to make sure I could get along with the person I signed a lease with.

I arrive to the apartment and she and her boyfriend, John, are there. John was nice, but he talked way too much. You're here to see Ashley, not me. I don't need to have a full conversation with you every time. There were times when he'd knock on my door about something.

BOY BYE.

Two days later, John leaves to go back home to Pennsylvania. Ashley and I decided to head to Marshall's to get bathroom and kitchen supplies. She had been crying since John left so it was a little awkward.

I bought paper towels and soap prior to getting to the apartment and told Ashley she can just get the next round of supplies. I also brought towels that I had freshly washed, pots and pans, and cups for communal use. It was very apparent that I had brought a lot more items to share than Ashley did.

A few days later I kept getting whiffs of weed from the apartment. I couldn't figure out where it was coming from. Was it our neighbors? Was it someone outside? Finally, I asked my roommate if she had been smelling the same thing. I knew it couldn't have been her.

> **Me:** *I've been smelling weed in our apartment like every day. Have you been smelling it? Do you think it's our neighbors?*
>
> **Ashley:** *Oh yeah, I've been smelling it, too. I have no idea where it's coming from.*
>
> **Me:** *So weird.*

A few days later, my friend Amber stayed overnight after a late night out and we both wake up to the smell of weed. Amber and I look at each other. I knew it was my lying roommate's ass cheifing in her room.

Here's the thing. I have nothing against people who choose to smoke weed. If I'm being honest, I myself have partaken in a few puffs here or there in my lifetime. What you're not going to do though is smoke it in my 480-square feet two-bedroom apartment that costs $3,100 a month. I wasn't in college anymore. If I were to bring a colleague over after work, I didn't want to have to worry about my apartment smelling like weed.

I had to address this now. I asked my friend to leave so that I could talk to Ashley without her feeling ganged up on. Ashley was in the shower, and I began scrubbing dishes in the sink like a psycho person trying to calm myself down. I was pissed for two reasons.

1. She had been smoking in our apartment since we moved in and not once asked me if I was OK with it.

2. She straight lied to my face. I was sharing all my belongings with her so the last thing I was going to let her do was disrespect me in my home.

The shower turns off. The door opens and I immediately address her.

> **Me**: *Ashley, have you been smoking in the apartment.*

She freezes.

> **Ashley:** *Yes. Sorry I was going to say something but I was scared.*
>
> **Me:** *Well, let me make it easy for you (This honestly was me being nice). I'm not OK with weed or any type of smoking in our apartment. I work too damn hard and spend too much on this place to have it smelling like weed. If your prerogative was to smoke weed in your home, you should have said something before we decided to live together. Are we on the same page?*
>
> **Ashley:** *Totally. It won't happen again.*
>
> **Me:** *Great.*

I texted her to confirm this as well so I had everything in writing. Weed smoking wasn't the only problem I had with Ashley. Ashley had some sort of misconstrued conception that household items appeared on their own. We had been without paper towels and dish soap for four days and Ashley never replaced it. I finally had to text her and ask her to pick up some. I didn't get it. This is when I questioned her childhood. How did her parents raise her? Not to mention she had this nasty stench to her. She always smelled sour. It was gross. I'm not even sure how often she showered.

It was the same thing with my new towels that I so nicely shared with her. I had them freshly washed when we moved in so we could both use them. A few weeks later they were over flowing in our bathroom dirty hamper for a week.

LIKE HELLO. Just because I was sharing with you did not mean I was going to pay to have them washed every time.

I texted her: Do you think you could have the towels washed?

I felt like her mother. It was so annoying. I had to tell her how to do everything.

With the dishes, I had to finally tell her that she needed to get her own. I bought two of everything when I went to Target thinking that if Ashley did the same we'd have four sets of everything. She never did so, I told her it was time.

With the cleaning supplies, Ashley finally got the hint that I thought she wasn't contributing enough so she bought a Swiffer, which was great. Unfortunately, she never used it. After living with Ashley for a year, I had not seen her clean the kitchen or bathroom once.

I legit did everything.

And just to add on to the laundry list of qualities Ashley did not possess, lack of consideration for others was also at the top of the list. I'd wake up to her yelling at her boyfriend via phone at 4:00 a.m. and calling him a pussy. I'd have to bang on the wall and remind her I was sleeping. This happened on several occasions.

A month after our first weed incident, I came home on a Friday night borderline tipsy from a happy hour with an old friend. Before I even opened the door I could smell weed. Our entire apartment reeked. I went from 0 to 100 real quick.

I came in and slammed the door. I could hear Ashley on the phone. I gave zero fucks.

> **Me:** *Ashley, can I talk to you?*

Ashley opens the door super meek.

> **Me:** *Why the fuck does our entire apartment smell like weed? I already told you how I felt about it. If my mom were to come surprise me and stay with me she wouldn't*

even be able to because of the smell. This is super disrespectful. I told you nicely once that I wasn't OK with this. If this happens again I will report you to the landlord.

She begins to cry.

Ashley: *Well, where am I supposed to smoke?*

I did not feel bad for her.

Me: *That has nothing to do with me. Figure it out because it will not be in here.*

Ashley: *It won't happen again.*

She goes back in her room.

I'm still fuming. I'm not done going off on her so I call my parents and talk shit about her loudly so she can hear everything I'm saying in our tiny apartment.

"Mom, she has no idea how crazy I am. I will report her ass so quick. This is not OK."

This goes on for about 30 minutes before I go into my room. I screenshot the section of the lease where it says no illegal substances and send it to her.

"Next time this happens I'm reporting you."

I felt like I was living out the lyrics of J.Cole's song "No Role Modelz": "Fool me one time, shame on you. Fool me twice, can't put the blame on you. Fool me three times, fuck the peace sign."

It was going to be World War III if it happened again.

Halfway through our lease, it actually happens again.

I come out my room and all I can smell is weed. I see a sheet stuffed under the door opening. I text her.

> **Me:** *Our apartment smells like weed again.*
>
> **Ashley:** *I went outside to smoke but some might have stuck on me when coming back in. But I'm sorry for the smell anyway.*
>
> **Me:** *To be honest, I really don't think that's what happened. Whenever you do bring the smell in, it's not that strong. You have sheet under your door again so that the smell doesn't come out. I really hope we don't have to go through this again because I will lose it.*
>
> **Ashley:** *It's not a sheet. They're pillows that fell off my bed because I was rearranging my room and putting down a new carpet. But I did take two hits inside. Blew it out the window. Didn't think it would smell so much, but clearly I was wrong. I've just been sick and didn't feel like going outside but that's not an excuse. I'm really sorry.*

This is when I realized Ashley must think I'm an idiot. She goes from lying to saying she's sick. She was a pathological liar and needed medication. This girl really needed help. She had no regard for me as her roommate.

> **Me:** *Are you fucking kidding me? I really hope you're joking. I can't live with you. Something needs to happen because I already told you what would happen if this happened again. You must think I'm an idiot. If you want to smoke so bad in your own home, move the fuck out and live with someone who is OK with it.*
>
> **Ashley:** *OK, I will start looking for someone to replace me and I will look for a new place to live.*
>
> **Me:** *Great.*

Three minutes later, Ashley starts knocking on my door crying. Mind you, it's 1:00 a.m. on a Saturday night and I'm in my pajamas watching TV in order to fall asleep.

I open the door with my resting bitch face.

" Can we talk or work something out? I can't afford to move."

I'm not really sure what else she said. I had zero cares in the world for Ashley.

I replied, "No, there's nothing else that can be done. You need to move out." I said this with zero emotion. She then starts yelping. Think of a two-year-old tantrum but in an adult. She began to say, "At least I opened the window" like if that was her way of being courteous.

It took everything in me not to laugh in her face. She didn't get it.

"Either move out or I report you," I said.

I closed the door. I had no desire to keep wasting my breath on her. She went back to her room, then she knocked on my door again five minutes later crying. I ignored her. I did not feel sorry for her. The next day, I contacted the leasing office about sublet logistics. I had them send her the paperwork. Now we just needed to find someone to replace her. Monday afternoon she sent me a text wanting to try and work things out. I told her it was too late. She should have thought about that the first time.

I come home that night after the gym and cook dinner. Ashley and her friend who looks about 18 years old walk in the apartment. Her friend is being extra nice to me and unusually chatty. She can tell I'm being stand-offish. She finally says, "So I know you and Ashley are dealing with some roommate challenges and I figured it would be a good idea for me to mediate and see if there's anything that can happen so that Ashley can stay in the apartment."

Just when I thought Ashley couldn't get any more delusional, she does. She brought over some random person to "Dr. Phil" us.

I said, "Look, I don't know you nor do I owe you an explanation as to what's going on in the apartment. What I will say is that Ashley has been given multiple chances and the next steps are her moving out or I report her."

I walk back into my room. This had to be a joke right? I overhear Ashley thanking her friend for trying. The next day I received an eight-page text from Ashley pretty much saying she's not moving and if I want to move I can.

The fuck?

Why would I be the one to move if I've followed the terms of lease from day one?

I called the leasing office letting them know the situation. They gave zero fucks. As long as they were getting their money on time, they didn't care what we were doing inside, even if it was a violation of the lease.

The next call I made was to the cops. Ashley needed to know I was serious about my threats. At 9:00 p.m., I saw the light come on in her room. I called the cops, and they arrived 15 minutes later.

They knock on the door and I let them in. They call Ashley outside her room and she looks like she saw a ghost. She has her phone in her hand and I can tell she's voice recording the conversation.

They ask her if she's smoking in her room and of course she says, "She's being crazy and making things up." It was like she grew a set of balls overnight because I knew damn well she would never be that bold if it was just the two of us. They split us up and I hear her crying to one of the cops. I was so tired of her crocodile tears.

The cop tells me they legally can't go in her room but that I could sue her in small claims court. They pretty much couldn't do anything.

They leave and my roommate follows behind them. I am beyond angry at this point. It took everything in me not to pick her up and shake the shit out of her. Putting your hands on someone is never the answer, but in that moment, I contemplated it. I contemplated it very hard.

Instead, I decided to re-affirm the fact that I was just as crazy as her delusional ass but in a different way. I wanted her to feel unconformable in her home—the same discomfort I was dealing with every time I walked into a marijuana-fumed, 480-square foot apartment. I turned off all the lights and waited for her ass to come back home to me just sitting in the dark.

She opened the door and jumped when she realizes I'm sitting on the couch.

The next day, she buys a bedroom door handle that locks and has moved her belongings including our microwave that are in the living room and kitchen in her room. I thought it was quite comical that she moved her Swiffer being that she had not used it once.

My mom, being the gem that she is, overnights a brand-new microwave to the apartment for my use. Gotcha bitch. I can play petty, too. I begin to move the one pot and the remainder of her minimal belongings in front of her door so that I can help her pack up.

The next morning, I realize Ashley has been using my dish brush and other belongings. I'll be damned if she thought she was going to move everything to her room so I couldn't use it but then still use my stuff.

I texted her.

> **Me:** *Do not use any of my belongings. This includes all kitchen supplies that I solely purchased.*
>
> **Ashley**: *It's a $5 brush. Are you kidding me?*

There she was being delusional again. How did she expect to still use my belongings after moving everything to her room?

> **Me:** *I don't care what it is. It's principle. Do not use it.*

Ashley loved to be bold via text but never in person.

I double text her.

> Me: *If you'd like to continue this conversation in person then we can do that.*

I got home the same time as Ashley and her boyfriend.

I came home hot and said, "So, like I told you via text do not let me have to tell you again about using my belongings."

Her boyfriend jumps in to tell me how childish I'm being.

I tell him calmly, "As soon as you pay rent your opinion will hold value. Until then, mind your own business."

"She pays more in rent than you."

"Well no shit. Her room is bigger."

"All you do is harass her and tell her what she needs to buy and not do."

I could no longer listen to this fool. I begin to raise my voice while doing the Black girl clap.

"But, *clap* do *clap* you *clap* pay *clap* rent?"

I repeated this statement five times. He couldn't get a word in. There was no way in hell I was going to let him disrespect me in my own home. The person who was a guest staying five days at a time and not paying utilities IN MY HOME.

Get the fuck out of my face.

My roommate doesn't say a word. They go back to her room as he yells, "You are crazy."

"Sure am! Lock your door tonight."

I go into my room and cancel her cable box and change the WiFi password. The cable was set up under my name and I had decided in that moment in time that I wanted to share nothing with her—not even if it cost me more money. I was petty with a capital "P."

The next day, I wake up at 6:00 a.m. for work and began blasting music, knowing they are both sleeping. When I returned home from work I realized she had been messing with the WiFi and had Time Warner, our internet provider, reset the login. I had to call Time Warner and go off on them. I told them that they needed to verify my identity before completing any changes from here on out. After receiving a credit and a sincere apology, I hung up the phone.

After a month of not speaking, awkward encounters, and back and forth with the WiFi and cable services she finally sends me at text that she has decided to move out if we're able to find a sublet to replace her.

CHALLENGE ACCEPTED.

It takes me five short days to find someone to replace her. We get as far as the request for the application and Ashley chokes. All of a sudden she doesn't have the money to move and didn't realize I would find someone to replace her so quickly.

I had no words. This girl was a child, which is something I already knew. I was more pissed that we involved poor Sarah who was more than ready to sign and put down her deposit to sublet Ashley's room. Not only that, but this time around it was Ashley's idea to move.

I apologized to Sarah for inconveniencing her, and Ashley and I went back to hating each other.

Before signing a lease with Ashley, it would have been impossible for me to even fathom being in a situation like this. I had the most perfect relationship with my roommate in Seattle, so much so that I ended up going to her wedding and gave a speech at her rehearsal dinner. She was amazing. We both cleaned. We both were considerate of one another. Yes, there were times where we'd get on each other's nerves, but that was normal. I remember I was in a bind one day at work and forgot my presentation on my USB at home. My roommate drove that day and she let me take her car to go get it. Other times when the two of us were traveling, we'd go and pick each other up from the airport. We genuinely enjoyed each other's company. I would regularly call my old roommate to bitch about my current one.

After 12 months of dealing with Ashley, it was finally time to move out.

I hadn't been at the apartment for about a day or so because I had partially moved into my new place already. I had some last-minute things to disassemble, clean up, and donate to charity. Ashley's boyfriend was of course in town. After two hours, I left the apartment quickly to drop some things off at Goodwill. I came back after being gone for literally 20 minutes and the apartment reeked of weed. I couldn't believe it. We had one last night in the apartment and she couldn't wait 12 more hours? I had someone coming to buy my couch later that night and was annoyed that the entire apartment smelled like weed. I paced back and forth as I start drafting revenge plans in my head. Technically, I wouldn't be sleeping there that night and all my belongings would be gone by the night since the leasing office walkthrough was the next morning. I hear my roommate and her boyfriend in her room laughing.

I decide on my revenge.

The girl buying my couch arrives. I apologize for the smell. She leaves. I grab the last of my things and put them outside the front door so I can make a quick get away.

I take the shower curtain and I take her entire bag of toiletries, which happened to be a raggedy Gap shopping bag containing fancy perfumes, lotion, creams, tampons, contacts, and soap. I call an Uber and dip. I ran out of my apartment with my last suitcase and a grin on my face.

I ask him to pull over once we cross over the bridge and I throw all her shit in a nearby garbage can. I figured she could use the money she saved on not buying anything to contribute to the household all year to upgrade her ghetto ass bag of toiletries.

I'm not saying what I did was right, but I am saying I was able to teach Ashley something my leasing office, two cops, and Ashley's random "Dr. Phil" friend couldn't— every action has consequences.

I was free. I immediately block her number. I had to see her one last time the next morning during the walkthrough and then I'd never have to see her trifling ass again.

I knew better than to get into another situation like that ever again. When searching for new roommates, my number one requirement was no recent college graduates. I explained the situation (providing the cliff notes of course) I was currently in. I made it very clear that I was not OK with smokers nor with someone who did not equally contribute to the apartment. I would never rush to make such an important decision on my living arrangements ever again.

LIFE LESSONS
FROM MY YEAR IN ROOMMATE HELL

- **You Must Have Self-Awareness**. If you are messy, own it and be upfront about it. It will save you the headache of a roommate bitching to you about it later on. If you painted the "I'm-a-perfect-roommate" picture, you are being dishonest with yourself and the other person. I personally couldn't live with a clean freak because I would annoy them. I'm known for leaving something in any room I enter whether it be a water bottle on the counter or a lipstick on the coffee table. It would drive that person insane.

- **Never Let Someone Live With You Without Being on the Lease.** This protects you. Let's say they had financial hardships and they are not able to pay rent. You pay the leasing office because they have your social security number. If you don't pay rent, you could be evicted and take a hit to your credit score. Your roommate needs to be equally responsible for rent being paid. If there's absolutely no way to add them on the formal lease, create a sublet agreement for them to sign. You can easily find a sample sublet lease online.

- **Ask for References and Social Media Handles**. Compare the opinions of the references to your potential roommates opinion of themselves. Are they similar? Did your potential roommate tell you they never go out, but their Instagram says otherwise?

To help you avoid my roommate nightmare, the next figure provides a list of questions to ask a potential roommate.

QUESTIONS FOR A
POTENTIAL ROOMMATE

Remember, this isn't a job interview. No questions are illegal. This is someone you will be living with for at least a year. Do your due diligence! Invasiveness does not exist when you are deciding whether or not to live with a stranger.

- [ ] Ask for their social media handles. This is important. If they are private, request them. Click on tagged photos and go through their friends' pages to see if they are all normal.

- [ ] Ask about income. Make sure they have a reliable source of income. Being a sugar baby is not an occupation. Check their LinkedIn profile. For New York apartments, you will need to know their salary to ensure your salaries combined make up more than 40% of the total year's rent.

- [ ] Ask about lifestyle preferences. Do they dance with Mary Jane? Do they have allergies to anything? Do they like pets?

- [ ] Ask about their work schedule. What is their work schedule like? Will you both be fighting over the bathroom in the mornings?

- [ ] Ask about significant others. Do they have a significant other? Do they invite random people back to their place?

- [ ] Ask about their age. This will give you a good sense of their maturity level and what stage of their life they are in.

- [ ] Ask about their plans after the lease expires. If all goes well, are they open to resigning? Or is there intent to move out at the end of lease and move across the country?

CHAPTER EIGHT

60/40: Evaluating Friendships

The older I get, the more often I contemplate the different relationships and friendships I have in life. Does this friendship benefit me? Do I spend more time annoyed or frustrated with this friend or do I enjoy their company? I also realized how much more I appreciated those friends who didn't make me feel bad for not speaking to them every day or every week. I was the closest to friends who I could call after not speaking for a month and it's like no time had passed. We're all busy. Your friends should understand.

Let's be clear. I'm not saying that if a friend calls you and you don't call them back, it's OK. It's actually not. If your ass has time to be on social media you have time to call or text someone back a "Hey, let's connect next weekend or this week instead" text.

When thinking about all the different friendships I had, I realized the easiest way to evaluate them all is something I call the 60/ 40 rule.

If this person annoys you 60% of the time you are either with or not with them, DROP THEM. This means that you only enjoy this friendship 40% of the time. This relationship is bringing no value to your life. Honestly, I had so many of these types of relationships. There were people in my life who leeched onto me because they were a friend of a friend or didn't have any other good friends geographical close to them. Not to say these people are bad people. Not everyone is meant to be friends and it's 100% normal to grow out of someone whom was once your best friend. People have varying personalities and that's what makes us all different.

Through and after college, our traits and personalities are ever changing. I remember my freshman year of college, I still hung out with all of my friends from high school. Since I went to a predominately White high school, all of my friends in college were also White. While there's nothing wrong with that, I knew that college was my opportunity to diversify my friend group. I wanted friends that understood and could relate to a lot of the experiences in life, both positive and negative, as an ethnic woman navigating another predominately White school. While I still kept in touch with a lot of my high school friends, I started hanging out with new people I met in my multicultural sorority and sometimes even intertwined my different friend groups.

During the navigation of new "friendlationships," there's going to be people with good, bad, and questionable intentions. Social media does this weird thing of making us all think we're friends with someone just because we follow each other on Instagram or are Facebook friends. I'm the first person to remind someone they don't know me.

I had this one friend named Michael in college who introduced himself to me through a mutual friend. Michael immediately got too comfortable. He's one of those guys who was beyond dramatic about any and everything. However, I accepted him for who he was. He would randomly call me to catch up post-college a few times a year.

A couple years later he decided he was going to relocate to New York. As soon as I found this out, I got nervous. He already had begun his crazy texting to me. If he texted me and I was at work and couldn't respond right away, I'd get a another text a couple hours later with a meme and a "Oh so you're not going to respond" text. Who did he think he was? I hate being nagged. He didn't get it. I even responded with an "I'm at work" text once and nothing changed.

When he finally moved to New York, it got worse. He assumed that everywhere I was he was supposed to get an invite to. He would screenshot my Instagram pictures and then send them to me with a comment like "Oh, really?" and an emoji with an annoyed face. Michael didn't get two things:

1. I obviously know what my Instagram photo looks like. I
    posted it.

2. If I wanted to invite you, I would have.

This kind of behavior drove me insane. Even after telling
him once again to stop sending me screenshots of my own
Instagram, he continued to do it. Instead of replying to his texts
with an attitude, I began to just ignore him. I was not going to
entertain his behavior. There were times I enjoyed his company,
but at the end of the day was it worth everything else?

I had another acquaintance I had met in college through a
good friend of mine named Tariq. Tariq loved to contact me
when he needed something. It wasn't a two-way street kind
of relationship. It wasn't like he reached out to me to see how I
was doing ever. Tariq was starting his own company and asked
me to help him with his mission statement. With everything I
had going on at the time, I don't know why I decided to help,
but I did. I don't even remember him thanking me. I never
heard anything about the company for about a year later. He
then sends a mass text to everyone in his phone book to send a
video to him for his promo video. This was another one of Tariq's
mistakes.

When asking people for unpaid help, one should, keep them in
the loop with the company or brand. Not once did Tariq send
me a message with a "Hey Baylie, thanks so much for helping
with the mission statement. Here's what's going on with the
brand right now."

You also have to personalize these requests. No one is going to want to help someone who receives a basic ass mass text. You're asking for someone to go out of their way to help you. The least you can do is send them a "Hey, how are you?" email before you put your hand out like a stripper after giving a lap dance.

With time, I have tried to become more patient in certain instances and scenarios. For example, in school I had only two relationships. Most of the time I was single. I used to always hate those girls that would drop everything for the guy they were dating. It was hard for me to understand. I used to get into arguments with my friends who would continually ditch me.

Today, I still have friends who prioritize their significant other over their friends, however the difference is my level of maturity. Once I acknowledged the fact that I couldn't change someone, I lowered my expectations. If my friend Tonya committed to something with me, I knew there was a 50% chance of her cancelling on me at the last minute. Once I lowered my expectations, I stopped caring as much and refrained from getting into unnecessary arguments. This was Tonya. I had known her for five years at this point. Did I love Tonya as a person? Yes. When I did hang out with Tonya, did I have a good time? Yes. It was because of her flakiness that I couldn't ever consider Tonya a close friend.

On the flip side, while I have become more patient in certain situations, there are specific characteristics and behaviors I will not tolerate, with disloyalty being one of these. As soon as I don't feel like you have my back, I'm done. If I can't trust you, I can't fuck with you. I refuse to have someone like that in my circle. This person would fall in the 60% of the 60/40 rule. If 60% of the time I'm wondering if you're going to fuck me over, that's too much work.

After a year of living in New York, a friend of mine named Gaby moved from Seattle to New York. I had been giving her advice on where to live, how to find roommates, and had introduced her to all of my friends since she didn't know a lot of people. She and my other friend Lauren hit it off and I was glad the three of us could all hang out together.

I'm not one of those possessive people who does not like their friends hanging out without them. There was a point in time where I began casually dating a new guy in New York at the same time my job had become overwhelming busy. I had less time to allocate across my friends, my time, and the new guy. I wasn't able to hang after work every day with Gaby and Lauren so they began hanging out frequently without me.

A few months later, the new guy and I fizzled out and work slowed down. I finally had more time to hang out. It was the first time the three of us had hung out in five weeks or so, but I couldn't help but feel left out. They had all these inside jokes and stories that I wasn't there for. Before leaving for the night, we decided we were going to all hang out at New York's annual SantaCon the next day. Gaby planned on starting early, but Lauren and I decided we wanted to work out, get our lives together, and then would head to meet Gaby together later on in the afternoon.

Around 11 a.m. I call Lauren to see what time she's heading to meet Gaby. She tells me she's already there.

Strange.

Lauren tells me to call her when I'm ready to leave and she'll tell me where they are. I start getting ready and leave my apartment 45 minutes later. I had two errands to run prior to meeting up with them. Around 2:00 p.m. I give them a call and can tell Gaby is already "turnt." She tells me they're about to go to another location and not to head that way until they get there. I try to figure out things to do to kill time in the interim. Forty-five minutes later and I still haven't heard from them. I text. No response. I text again. No response. I call. No answer.

Twenty minutes later, they finally call me back and tell me to meet them at some bar in Lower East Side. I get in an Uber and head that way. At this point, I had spent 90 minutes trying to kill time and was royally annoyed. My Uber is close and I text Gaby letting her know I'm almost there. She responds saying they're leaving and going somewhere else now. I ask her if she can just stay put for a few minutes because I'm almost there. She says she can't because she's with a big group of people. What the fuck?! If Gaby and Lauren were real friends they could have waited for a supposed good friend for five minutes. After

20 more minutes of this and having to get out of my Uber and walk to the other bar, I finally meet up with them. It had taken a total of 2.5 hours for me to meet up with them.

I couldn't believe I let that much time go by. I get there and realize something is off. Gaby's friend Patrick is there. I realize Gaby is trying to set up Patrick with Lauren, even though Gaby was present when Patrick and I had hit it off a few months prior.

I ask her, "Hey are you trying to set up Patrick and Lauren?"

She responds, "I'm not trying to do anything. That's pure chemistry, OK?" with a certain tone in her voice.

This rubbed me the wrong way. Even if the Patrick thing didn't happen, I had decided in the car that I was done with them. We didn't have one of those immature friendship breakups where we unfollow each other and talk shit. I simply just didn't want them in my circle anymore and that was that. I had so many great friends already, so why force something with someone when you don't have to?

Just as easy as it can be to walk away from a short-lived friendship as the above situation was for me, our ego can sometimes makes us think it's just as easy to walk away from a long or extremely meaningful friendship. These are the people that will teach you patience. These are the people that will teach you forgiveness. These are the people that pass the 60/40 test with flying colors. No one is perfect. Your friends will inevitably do something that will piss you off or something you'd never do. Now that you're an adult, you can use your words in a leveled tone of voice. Pick an appropriate time and place and have these conversations in private. Let them know how the situation made you feel and if that person cares about you like you do about them, they will listen, share their point of view, and you both can hopefully move on.

Surround yourself with people with big hearts, ambitions, similar interests, and loyalty. Your friends are your support group outside your family. They will hold you accountable. They will tell you if you have lipstick on your teeth or a bat in the cave. They will help you when you're in need. The friendships I have kept after college are the ones that are most meaningful to me. While college has its moments, it's the post-college trials and tribulations that have really tested and proven my friendships until this day.

When you think about it, during college you are still figuring out who you are. It's hard for you to narrow down exactly what you expect of other people in your friendships when you're still discovering you. Think about the traits and characteristics you want in a friend. In the next figure, I've included some of mine to help give you an idea.

FIGURE 8

QUALITIES OF A GOOD FRIEND

As you evaluate your post-college friendships, here are some good traits and qualities to keep in mind.

QUALITIES AND TRAITS	EXAMPLE
Communicative	Let me know when I do something that bothers you. Don't hold it in!
Non-judgmental	Give me advice while not judging me for some of the poor/ thot-like decisions I've made in life.
Fun	Can I have a good time with you with no alcohol, with alcohol, with no one around, and in group settings?
Loyal	Will you have my back? Don't choose when and when you don't want to be my friend.
Ambitious	Have goals of your own. Challenge me when I'm not pushing myself hard enough. It inspires me to continue to be my best self.
Confident	Be comfortable in the person you are. Don't always seek affirmation from others to make decisions in your life.
Trustworthy	Can I tell you something and be sure you won't purposefully run your mouth or attempt to sabotage me?

FIGURE 8.2

What are the qualities and traits that are important
to you? Use the chart below to list those qualities
and examples.

QUALITIES AND TRAITS	EXAMPLE

Isn't it funny how all of the traits above are expectations
you have set for yourself well? Once I figured out what was
important to me in my friendships, I weeded out the people
who didn't make the 60/40 rule cut.

LIFE LESSONS
LEARNED FROM POST-COLLEGE FRIENDSHIPS

I'm Too Damn Old to Force Any Type of Friendship. I'm not going to be friends with someone to just to say or tell other people we are. If we don't vibe, we don't vibe and that is OK.

If Someone Is Important To You, Swallow Your Pride, Put Aside Egos, and Have a Conversation About It. Don't hold it in to passively bring up a few months later when they do something to piss you off. If you need to establish guidelines do that. Let's say there's a certain topic or person neither of you can agree on, agree to refrain from discussing it or that person with each other.

Be a Ride or Die. If you are a ride or die for others, they will ride out for you too.

Eliminate Toxic Friendships or Friendships That Require Too Much Work. Again, remember that the good in any relationship should significantly outweigh the bad.

If You're in a Relationship, Make Sure to Carve Out Time For Your Other Friendships. These friends will be the ones left picking up the pieces if you ever dump their ass.

CHAPTER NINE

Single AF

---

*"Whoever did Voodoo on my love life
can chill now. I learned my lesson."*

–Unknown

*"It takes a strong person to remain
single in a world that is accustomed to
settling with anything just to say they
have something."*

–Unknown

*"Occupations of majority of the men
that hit on me: bus driver, subway rider,
construction worker, and homeless."*

–Baylie Robinson

When it comes to relationships, my greatest fear is not ever being loved. My greatest fear is finding that person I want to give my heart and soul to and it not be reciprocated. How do you commit to just one person with all of the temptation at your fingertips? How do we feel comfortable and 100% trusting in the relationship we're in? To be honest with you—this is getting a little philosophical and I'm clearly not the right person to be giving dating advice. I am as single as Martha Stewart was on her prison release day. What I can provide you with is the many comedic stories (and learnings!) being single has provided me with.

I don't care what anyone says, but the relationship a daughter has with her father truly affects how she views and interacts with men. I've seen my father cry once my entire life. I think my father assumed that we just knew he loved us because that's how normal fathers were supposed to feel. I wasn't raised being told "I love you" every day. He didn't give me 10 dollars just because I wanted it. I didn't receive an answer just because I asked. My father liked to tell us to "Figure it out." I learned to be independent and self-sufficient.

At one point in life a third party was suing me. I consulted my father about the situation. He gave me his point of view and advice and he simply said, "OK you're on your own." He refused to do the work for us. I found a lawyer who took my case on contingency and I actually won my case. A part of me felt better that I had done the research and won on my own without daddy's help.

While there were many great inherited qualities, traits, lessons, and home-cooked meals from my father, he wasn't necessarily someone I could confide or find comfort in until my mid-20s. Though my father eventually got softer with age, it's still so hard for me to be vulnerable or be open with men. You know how some people start with the glass full or half empty? My glass starts empty. Like I can see my reflection in the bottom kind of empty. There are pieces of my life I will only disclose once I can fully trust you. The same goes for basic friendships. It's easier for me to be an asshole because once I deeply care about someone it's inevitable for me to get hurt. In the next figure, you can see some statistics about today's dating environment.

FIGURE 9

MODERN-DAY DATING STATISTICS

The median age at first marriage is

27 & **29**

for women   for men

versus 1960s median age of 20 for women and 23 for men

Marriage Rates are Expected to Drop for the following groups

70% Millennials   **91%** Boomers

87% Late Boomers   **82%** Gen-Xers

25% of millennials are likely to never be married

Roughly **25%** of unmarried young adults (between 25-34) are living with a partner.

Dating in Seattle was an absolute joke for me. It was like God put all of my "Not types" in one city. I figured, why not see what all the dating app hype was all about?

EXPERIMENTING WITH DATING APPS

Tinder was the first dating app I ever tried and Jordan was the only Tinder date I ever went on in Seattle. Here's what I learned from Jordan: The amount of money in a man's wallet is subsidiary to his heart. It took me 90 minutes to realize how big of a tool this guy was. I should have known better and swiped to the left but I was intrigued that a NFL player needed a dating app to meet women. After an exchange of multiple Tinder messages, I gave him my number.

Strike one.

He texted me a "This Jordan" text. At the age of 22, decent grammar wasn't too much to ask for, right? That was his first strike. We figured out a time and place to meet. I freshly washed and blow dried my hair. I wanted to make sure I looked as good as possible.

He lived 30 minutes from me and he suggested we meet at a restaurant five minutes from his place. This also bothered me, but I let it go. I was on my way to our date and was getting more anxious by the second. I hadn't been on a date since I moved to Seattle and my first one was with an NFL player. Jordan asked me to text him when I was five minutes away and I still made it there before him. I think he did that on purpose to make an entrance.

Strike two.

Overall, I'd rate his appearance a 5 out of 10. He wasn't my usual type. We hugged and he asked me if I wanted to sit at the bar or get a table. I suggested the bar. We sat down and both ordered a drink. He ordered a Hennessey on the rocks and I ordered a Prickly Pear Margarita. College football happened to be on and he split his gaze between the two of us. I started to ask him questions about himself in order to get to know him better. He would answer and there would be no reciprocal response. This went on for about 20 minutes. I found out he was from California, had three siblings, was a communications major, and broke up with his ex because she was a cheating "ho." During this time, he only found out where I went to school and how old I was. I gazed off and sighed. He had no interest in getting to know me at all. His phone began to ring and he had the audacity to answer it.

Strike three.

I sat there fuming beside him. It was one of his teammates calling. It felt like a 10-minute phone call. At this point, I knew I never wanted to see him again and gave no fucks how he perceived me. I looked at my phone and told myself I'll give this guy 30 more minutes of my time. He apologized once he hung up. In my head I thought, "Too late."

We began talking again and I asked him what kind of girls he usually dated. I don't quite remember his full response but I do remember one part word for word. He replied, "I know I look and dress good, and I need someone who takes pride in how they look, too." I immediately looked him up and down and stared at his entire outfit, which I'd like to call Gucci cannibalization. He had on a Gucci belt, a Gucci T-shirt, and Gucci sneakers and really thought he was doing something. Black people always try to act like they know how to dress because they have two pieces of designer apparel that they wear all together. I responded with a mumbled "interesting."

He then suggested I come back to his place so we could sit by his fireplace and drink wine. His exact words were "You wanna come over to my place so we can sit by my fireplace and drink whatever is that stuff y'all girls like?" I had been in the game too long to not know that Jordan was trying to be slick.

I said, "You just met me for the first time, and you're inviting me to your place? This was the first thing I said with an attitude the entire date.

He said, "Yeah, why not? If you end up being crazy I'll just kick you out."

Strike 453879.

I was so done. I couldn't believe that I had subjected myself to 90 minutes with this fool. I had way too much of an ego to let a professional athlete mistake me for a jump off. "Well, it was nice meeting you. I actually have to run to Costco to get my tires looked at before they close." I deleted Tinder as soon as I got in my car and never spoke to him again.

Five months later, I ran into him at a house party and neither of us said a word to each other. I'm glad we were on the same page.

MEETING ON INSTAGRAM

Bored with my whopping number of zero options in Seattle, I began talking to Daniel. He was my "What if" guy. You know everyone has one.

Daniel attended the nearby university to mine. I always knew who he was in college, but I never actually met him in person before. He was 100% my type. I randomly followed him on Instagram a year after graduation. He followed back shortly after. I thought, why didn't I ever make a move prior to moving across country? Months later, I wake up to a slew of Instagram notifications. Daniel decided to go on a liking spree on my page I returned the favor. Daniel proceeds to comment on a picture I posted nine months prior.

"Text me."

Well alrighty then.

After five months of talking, we finally meet in person in Atlanta. I was nervous but had luckily had a few drinks of courage in me. I liked Daniel before I met him, but as soon as I saw him in person, I knew I really liked him. Our chemistry was insane. I so desperately wished we lived in the same city. Knowing he was going back to Florida while I was flying back to Seattle killed me. How was I just supposed to forget about the entire weekend?

Months went by and we continued talking frequently. His birthday was coming up and I had brought up how I wanted to visit San Francisco to visit a friend and would love to see him while I'm there. He was from an area a few hours outside the area and had moved home temporarily before going into his training course for work in Georgia. He had plans to go to Vegas with his buddies first and then planned on meeting me in San Francisco after. The day of his birthday, I sent him a text before I left for the airport. It read, "Happy Birthday Daniel. I hope you have an amazing birthday with your friends! Just make sure you make it out alive to see me in San Francisco. Can't wait to see you!"

Frankly, I really didn't care what him and his friends got into in Vegas. Him and I were not in a relationship and I was perfectly fine with that. I still got to do my thing while he got to do his. I never worried about any other girl because he was never my man to worry about.

He responds to my text right away.

> *"Thanks Baylie! I will try to make it out alive. I'm not sure if I'll make it to San Francisco anymore. My friends aren't wanting to go there from Vegas."*

This is where I subside the attitude in me.

> **Me:** *What? Isn't it your birthday? Shouldn't they do what you want to do?*
>
> **Daniel:** *Haha, you right! I'll talk to them.*

I didn't care if he had to walk to San Francisco from Vegas. If he didn't make it there, I was done. I was tired of wasting my time having a mobile relationship. He had an opportunity to see me without even having to fly anywhere and he was going to miss the opportunity. He texts me a few hours later asking how my trip was going.

ignore

Unless he was texting me to make arrangements to San Francisco, I had nothing to say to him. The petty person in me began snap-chatting, so he knew I was ignoring his ass. He was the first person to watch every single one.

A day later he texts me again, "What's the name of your hotel?"

Got him! It could have been so much easier if he made the decision on his own. He rented a car and booked a hotel room that night where I was staying. He arrived that night with one of his friends. The two of us decided to go to Twin Peaks at 3 a.m. I was freezing until he grabbed an extra jacket in his car to put on me. We stood outside the car and overlooked the city for hours. I still don't understand how I felt so strongly for someone I barely knew. We went home and I stayed in his room. I don't even like to cuddle, but somehow I loved every minute being next to him. We both left the next day and that was it. We went through the same motions until it died. I felt like I lost a best friend, but I had too big of an ego to say anything.

A few months later, I received a plus one to a good friend's wedding. The only person I wanted to take was him. I knew

Daniel lived within driving distance of the wedding venue. After a week of back and forth, I finally decided to ask him. Daniel unknowingly taught me how to put myself out there and take risks not knowing the outcome. I was so used to men pursuing me that I had never been put in a position where I had to make an effort. I was scared he would say no.

He responded back and said he would love to go if he could get the time off of work. With the wedding being at 5:00 p.m. on a Sunday, he'd have to get the following Monday off. Unfortunately, they wouldn't approve the time off and he had to report in at 5:00 a.m. that morning. There was no way I'd have him do that. I was sad, but I was reassured that he still cared enough to want to come to the wedding with me.

At that point, I went back to my daily routine. My intent was never to go back into the talking every day thing we had done on and off so many times. He began initiating conversation more and here we were again. He had never been to New York before and since we both loved Drake, he decided to plan a trip to visit me the weekend of his concert. I was so anxious to see him that I brought up the idea of going to Atlanta for the Fourth of July. He told me he only had plans one day to go to Six Flags but that was it. Six Flags is always there, but a pretty girl coming to visit you isn't. I was so confused how Six Flags was even a factor. I told him I'd make plans that day with other friends. I drunkenly Face Timed him the next day (I was at boozy brunch, OK? Don't judge me.) He told me if I got my flight he'd get us a hotel in the city. He just needed to confirm when he was going to Six Flags.

Again, with the motherfucking Six Flags.

Daniel also taught me patience. I let him get away with shit I'd never let any guy get away with. If it was any other guy I would have dropped their ass a long time ago. With him, I tried to talk things out rather than just walking away.

Next thing I know Daniel and I are getting into it about Six Flags. I was the only one getting heated. Daniel was a chill guy. He hated confrontation and didn't know what to do when I would call him out on things. He kept changing his plans regarding Six Flags and I took this as him not wanting me to go. It was more than just Six Flags for me. I felt like this was just another example of Daniel never making me a priority. He never let me get close enough for us to get anywhere. There was always something else that was way more important.

I realized this two months later when he made the Face Time call to break the news that his job wasn't letting him leave base to come to New York. I knew he had no control over that instance, but it was the Domino effect of it all. I couldn't do it anymore. I wanted nothing more than to get to a place with him where we could build a relationship and be together. I loved myself enough to walk away. Daniel and I couldn't just be friends so there was no point even trying.

If you're wondering what I did with his ticket, ask the scout outside Madison Square Garden who bought it off me. And no, I did not give Daniel his money back. I pocketed that shit.

The next figure provides you with some of my tips for developing a great online dating experience. Remember, if no one has ever told you this before, I'm going to be the one to tell you—You are damn sure worth the wait.

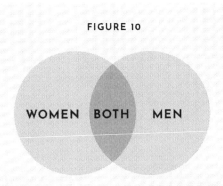

FIGURE 10

WOMEN BOTH MEN

THE DO'S & DON'TS
FOR ONLINE DATING

WOMEN	BOTH	MEN
Include a mix of selfies and action shots of yourself and with friends.	List your job title.	Include photos that are clear and easy to identify who you are.
Be versatile with your looks. If you go back and forth between wearing your hair curly and straightening it, show photos of you rocking both.	Complete the *about me* section. Invite a close friend to review and sign off on your profile.	Don't include photos with other women unless it's clear that the woman is a relative Don't include photos with sunglasses on. Women will assume you have something to hide.
Once you make a connection, don't be afraid to initiate plans.	Choose a public place for your first meeting.	Limit your bathroom and mirror selfies. Be respectful with initiating your opening communication.

TO GHOST OR NOT TO GHOST

It didn't take me long to want to get back in the game. I re-downloaded the Bumble dating app. The guys were way better looking and most men seemed to be doing something with their lives. The concept of messaging first was too much pressure for me. Was this how guys feel when they text you for the first time after getting your number? I'd spend so much time contemplating what to say first that I'd just give up and not send anything.

There were a few guys I did end up meeting from the app. The first one was a guy named Michael who didn't actually live in New York. He was from Miami and was in New York for a business trip. I was giving him recommendations of places to go visit. After a few hours of conversation, we realized we both had the same Saturday night plans. We were both going to a nightclub on top of Dream Hotel. We exchanged numbers and made plans to link up with each other on Saturday night. My girlfriend, Lauren, came with me as we walked in the hotel lobby a little after 12:30 a.m. I text him the "Hey, I'm here" text and he comes down two minutes later. I immediately froze. This mothafucker looked NOTHING like his pictures. I can tell it's him but with like 50% more acne and 30% less height. He must have seriously "Face tuned" his pictures because he was not what I came there for.

He gave me a hug and asked how our night was going. I was nice and said, "So nice to meet you. We're gonna go to the bathroom, but will be right back." You already know what happened next. We dipped. Uh, taxi please? I ran so fast out the front door I nearly knocked over the 300-pound security guy myself.

In retrospect, I definitely could have handled this better, but in my eyes it was false advertisement on his end. After telling this story to my close friends, I received a handful of opinions all stemming from the same piece of advice. If you're being told from your friends that your standards are too high, really take a step back and think about what you're looking for. After being told this for years I realized my friends were absolutely wrong. Because I haven't found the right guy, I have to lower my standards? I was only looking for things in men that I equally brought to the table, such as education, attraction, a good job, and a long-term plan.

My second Bumble experience wasn't as bad. He was a lawyer from my hometown of Orlando. He lived in the East Village not far from where I was living at the time. He was, 5'9, 27-year-old, and Indian. He was adamant about taking me out. I had to cancel our first planned date and then he followed up to reschedule. I was 10 minutes late and as soon as I met him, I knew it wasn't going to go anywhere. He really was a nice guy, but there was no spark or connection. He had this lame kind of walk that encompassed a shimmy of the shoulders. We grabbed a table outside, me sitting in the booth, him taking the chair. The conversation didn't really flow. There were several awkward pauses in the conversation and I felt like I had to take the lead at driving the conversation. I love when a man takes charge of the conversation and takes the initiative to ask questions. It shows he's genuinely interested in getting to know you.

Normally, I've been known to drink a lot on a date. It helps loosen up my nerves. However, this date I wanted no more than two drinks so that it could be over.

After the first drink, he mentioned that we could go to another spot afterwards unless we wanted to stay there. I insisted we just stay there for a second drink. I really had no desire to go to another spot with him. After the second drink, we left the bar and walked in the direction of both of our homes. We got to my cross section and I thanked him for the night and went in for a hug. He went in for a kiss and I awkwardly turned my body so that it wouldn't happen. Did he think the night went that well that a kiss was warranted?

The next day I received a text from him wanting to solidify another date for us to link up. The old Baylie would have just not responded. A good friend of mine recently advised against this type of behavior. He made me realize how important it was to give someone closure and to just be honest. Letting someone play the "what did I do wrong" game is mean. Everyone deserves some type of closure.

I'm not talking about a five-paragraph text listing the reasons as to why you can't be with someone. First off, if you have any inclination to send a five-paragraph text, you need to either call or arrange to meet that individual in person because you obviously feel stronger for that person than you realize.

I've been on the other side of receiving a five-paragraph "I'm not feeling this text" and it confused me more than anything. Leave it to me to receive a break-up text while not even having a boyfriend.

I did end up sending this guy a text. It simply said, "Hey, it was good to finally meet you. I just wanted to be honest in the fact that I don't see this going any further than friends. Thank you again for taking me out last night and enjoy the rest of your week." Plain and simple. Some guys respond and some don't. As long as you did your part you don't have to worry about Karma coming to find you again later.

My third most memorable Bumble experience is quite comical. This is the moment in life where I truly contemplated giving up on men, moving to Vermont, and working on a cow farm.

His name was Sean. He was also from my hometown and went to the same high school as me four years prior. We had nine mutual friends, so I was hopeful that this could be something that could be promising. We did a few of the back and forth basic messages.

> **Me:** *Did you have a good Fourth or was waking up for you as big of a struggle as it was for me?*

(You see that game I'm spitting, right?)

> **Sean:** *It was good but, I only got 4 hrs of sleep. I just moved into a Sprinter van and I left the vent open while at The Marina so things got a little wet.*

Me: *confused emoji* What?

Mind you, I had to google what a Sprinter Van actually was before responding.

Sean: *Yep.*

Me: *Why are you living in a van?*

I don't even know why I was still responding at this point, but now I was intrigued.

Sean: *Tired of paying rent.*

Me: *I feel like I'm being punk'd.*

Sean: *I swear. My snap and instagram = Mistervanhattan.*

Clever.

Sure enough, he wasn't lying. I swear I can't make this shit up. He really lived in a van. I couldn't even deal. It wasn't even like he had a lot of followers and this was a big movement or something.

At this point, I'm freaking out. Like I know this was a decision he made by choice and that's fine. I'm sure there are women out there who are OK with this lifestyle. I was not. I'm not even OK with staying in a damn hostel. Poor guy had no shot. How could I date a guy who didn't believe in paying rent when I owned shoes more than 55% of my monthly rent? I'm not saying money is everything, but let's practice self-awareness.

Sean: *Did you verify?*

Me: *I did.*

Sean: *And?*

Me: *Now I believe you!*

Sean: *Ha! Fair enough!*

Dating Apps Can Be Tough For a Number of Reasons (Yet, I'm Still on Them):

1. **Vibes**. My friends make fun of me for this, but I honestly believe in the importance of a spark or a flowing connection with someone. How are you supposed to pick up on someone's vibes through a dating app?

2. **Flirting.** Flirting or being intriguing while messaging a person you've never met before can be hard especially if you hate small talk like me. Personally, half of the guys I was messaging at the time had no idea they were messaging Jarryd, my gay best friend, and not me. I had gotten to the point where I'd just hand Jarryd my phone and he knew what to do.

I was so much better in person. Guys on Bumble weren't always keen on having good conversation and then arranging a time and day to meet up. I wasn't about to waste three more days of my life entertaining mindless how was your day conversation with a person I had never physically seen with my own eyes. After a successful first conversation surrounding the basics of the workplace, family, hobbies, and hometown, I would have been so down to just grab a drink with one of them.

3. **Handling Uncertainty.** I don't think anyone can handle a "Surprise! This is what I looked like on Bumble, but this is real life" or the "Well self-employed really means I live in my grandma's mother in law suite for zero rent."

I know that we're supposed to take risks in love and relationships but I had started to consider asking for scanned copies of each guy's W-2 upon receiving the first message. "Um, sir are you able to provide a form of identification and a signed copy of your W-2 for verification purposes? It would have saved me time and wasted conversations with my friends regarding what to say back.

A BAD CASE OF ER

Aside from dating apps, the other challenge in today's dating is the fact that some of us are blinded by a Bad Case of ER. You could potentially miss out on a great partner because there's someone else who:

- Is rich(er)

- Is pretti(er)

- Has a fatt(er) ass

- Has long(er) hair

- Comes from a bett(er) family

- Has bigg(er) breasts

- Lives in a nic(er) neighborhood

I can't tell you how many times I've been left for someone else. Someone else who apparently had more of that something. Sometimes that "someone else" was an actual other person and sometimes that "someone else" was a fiction of their "who else is out there" imagination.

TWO THINGS CAUSE A BAD CASE OF ER

- Ego

- Social Media

Have you ever been in a relationship with someone during their turning point? Let's say you met them at a very low point in their life. Let's say you were there for them during these hard times and helped them emotionally or financially through it. Let's say you were with them when they were 50 pounds heavier. Eventually they hit the tip of their bell curve. This could mean that financially, physically, and professionally they hit a high moment in their lives and decide they can do better and need to upgrade. Social media makes it even easier for us to make these ill-informed comparisons of what else is out there.

My mom once told me, "If you spend your entire life comparing yourself to others, you will always be miserable." She's right per usual.

Many of the people I follow or who follow me are getting engaged, are already married, or have one to a helluva lot of kids. You're on your own timeline. As much as I told myself I needed to be married with kids by 30, if it doesn't happen, it doesn't happen.

LIFE LESSONS
FROM DRAKE ON DATING

Looking back on the men I've had relations with, I've discovered, with the help of Aubrey Drake Graham, Four mottos and lessons every single woman or man should remember in his or her dating journey.

1. **Mothafuckas never loved us.** Every asshole wanted us to think they did. If they really loved you, they would have never screwed you over or put you in the position in the first place. They wanted you to think they did right before you slept over for the first time. I've personally heard so many excuses in my life that I could write a sequel to this book titled "Sorry Ass Excuses Written By The Man You Thought Was Your Man."

I've learned to never invest in any person until at least six months of consistent behavior. Think about it. The first month of talking to a new guy or gal is super exciting. You're both super attracted to each other with this chemistry that you're still figuring out. You're eager to know more about this person while disclosing as much as you're comfortable in sharing. The small burst of happiness you feel when you get that "How was your day" text. It's OK to be excited about a new fling, but make sure you are treading slowly. I never really understood those girls who were cooking and cleaning for a guy who wasn't actually their boyfriend. I've never had a man even ask me to cook for him.(This may be because my cooking is subpar. But still.)

2. **You lose some and win some.** Long as the outcome is income. You're allowed to be upset after any relationship. We're human. It's what you do and the decisions you make afterwards determine where you go next. Do not use the next two weeks of your life eating ice cream. Does this person dictate the number you see on your paycheck? They sure don't. You will survive. Take this as a learning lesson for next time. Are these the type of people you should be avoiding? Should you wait longer until becoming intimate with someone in order to make sure they are someone you really could be with? I've learned something from every guy I've ever been with. That's why when I run into guys from my past they get that "pat pat" hug and I keep it moving. Nothing kills them more than you acting like they are irrelevant. Close that chapter in your life and move on. The best revenge is you living your life. Get that promotion, find you a fine ass (wo)man, and continue to post your bad bitch Instagram photos.

3. **Cause you're a good girl (or guy) and you know it**. "You is beautiful. You is smart. You is kind." Know your self worth. Do not let someone's Stage 5 ER condition start making you think this is your fault. I've been down this path right after receiving the "Let's be friends text." Don't do it. I've had many short-term "dating and talking" relationships and not one of them made me doubt the person I was. Remind yourself how much you have to offer and channel

that energy into something or someone actually worth your time.

4. **Karma's such a thing of beauty.** If one thing is certain, it's this: They ALWAYS come back. It may not be right away, but they eventually do. Even men who ended it with me still crept up later on in life. I have guys from my past still texting me while having girlfriends. This goes back to my point of moving on and focusing on you. People are intrigued by things they can't have. My focus on being successful, looking my best, and being happy with my own self was contagious. It killed some of these people who were once sleeping in the same bed next to me to know that I no longer gave any fucks about them. I can tell you right now that each of these people know what city I currently reside in, the field I'm working in, my current relationship status, and the last vacation I went on without me directly providing this information. Don't let them fool you. They are peeping your every move. Remember, karma comes in all shapes and sizes. Some were served weight gain of 20 or more pounds, some were served with an unexpected pregnancy from a random girl they met at a local bar, and others were served with silence after they hit send on their "You up?" text.

PART THREE

Staying True to Yourself

CHAPTER TEN

Loving You First and Doing It Well

Your 20s are a pivotal point in your life. We grow and we change. You will not be the exact same person you were on graduation day and that's perfectly OK. You may not have all the same friends. You may not be dating the same person. You may or may not fit in the same jeans. I like to think that with each year, we are a newer and better version of ourselves. If those experiences were positive, how can we ensure they will be a recurring part of our lives? If those experiences were negative, how can we learn and avoid them going forward?

LEARN HOW TO BE SELFISH

Selfish: lacking consideration for others; concerned chiefly with one's own personal profit or pleasure.

For a moment, I want you to remove the negative connotation pre-programmed in your brain surrounding the word selfish. If all of society defined the world selfish simply as "putting yourself first" or in simpler words, how would you feel about it? Would your actions change?

For example, before my decision to make my move to New York, I struggled with the fact that I'd be ditching my friend and Seattle roommate who had just moved in four months prior. I felt guilty knowing she had packed up her life to live with me and I would be leaving just shortly after. However, what sense would it had made to stay miserable and depressed in a city solely because I didn't want to inconvenience a roommate? I had to make my New York move for me. I had to be selfish and put my needs first. Part of being an adult is making tough decisions and this happened to be one of them. Was I fucking her over and not paying my rent through the end of the lease? No. I'm not a complete asshole. I gave her notice and paid rent until the end of the lease even though I was not living there. I prioritized myself while still honoring my commitments.

You need to keep the same prioritizing yourself mentality in the workplace as well. Let's say your dream job opens up at your company. Your best friend at work tells you how excited they are about applying for the position. Would you still apply?

The answer better be HELL YES.

If it isn't, I want you to ask yourself why you'd suppress yourself from your own dreams so someone else can get closer to theirs?

When you say it out loud, it sounds quite absurd doesn't it?

One thing I like to do to prioritize myself on a weekly basis is weekly me time. Anyone who knows me knows I'm on the far end of the extrovert spectrum. I love to be out and about. I love being out with friends. I love talking. However, I try to make time to be alone throughout the week. Whether that alone time is in my room watching my favorite show, writing a blog post for my blog, The Baysics, going for a run, or simply self reflecting. During my me time I do not feel bad ignoring calls or not responding to text messages. It's time I set aside for myself to mentally decompress. It's how I can ensure I can be my best self in everything else I do.

LIFE LESSONS
ON PUTTING YOURSELF FIRST

- **Stop Comparing Yourself to Others.** I'll admit, being selfish is easy, but this one is a hard one that I continue to struggle with. Social media has made other's personal and professional lives easily accessible and easily comparable. Stacy got engaged last week. Laura got a promotion this month. Jonathan is having a baby. Luis just bought a brand new Mercedes. Christina just got a new puppy. We all showcase what we want people to see on social media. It's just what we do. You think I was going to make a post about getting fired at work? Nahhhhh.

Life isn't a competition. Life isn't about who gets where first or gets there last. It's about doing what makes you happy with people who make you happy all in due time. While it's great to have goals set for ourselves, we also need to understand how to readjust if we don't accomplish them and re-asses those goals in the first place. Do you really want to be married right now or is it because five of your friends just recently got engaged?

Do you really want to leave your job to get a senior title because you're ready or because someone else you know just got promoted at his or her job? The decisions and actions you make should solely revolve around you and only you. If you think you can convince a manager you're worthy of a pay raise because Sharon, who's been at the company as long as you have just got a raise, you're highly mistaken. Don't let social media or water cooler conversations ever let you forget that.

·   **Accept the Cards You Are Dealt.** This essentially ties to the above. A lot of us like to make excuses for why other people got to where they are in life, such as "She came from money," "His dad owns the company so that's how he got the job," "She's super skinny naturally and doesn't even work out,"

"His parents paid for his college tuition, so he doesn't even have student loans to pay off," or "She's mixed so she has good hair." We get it. The grass is always greener on the other fucking side. Deal with it. Life sometimes sucks. As soon as you come to terms with the aspects of life that are irreversible and cannot be changed, you will be able to focus on the aspects of your future that are yet to be written.

· **Treat Yo Self.** This is an important one. For some of us, this may come naturally while for others it may be a foreign concept. Express self-love through a small or big gesture, depending on your budget. Take a vacation. Splurge an extra $10 at the nail salon to get a chair massage. Save up for the designer pair of shoes you've been wanting. Buy a ticket to your favorite artist's concert. Make a reservation at your fave restaurant. We all work hard (well, hopefully you do!) but we don't work just to work. We all have a purpose for why we work. Your reasoning may be to make enough to support your parents, to buy a house, to help people, or to save lives.

If you start doing the above three things, you'll notice how less and less you care about what others think about you. You'll start living your life for you. Everyone is given one life and this is yours only. Publishing a book has been a goal of mine for years. The road to publishing is not an easy one and there were times where I questioned if I could do it and if the work and money I was putting into it was worth it. While working on this book, an editor I had hired at the time, advised me I needed to launch a blog in the interim in order to showcase my writing style prior to my book and establish a social presence. My first thoughts were "Everyone has a blog and I don't want to do what everyone else is doing." I also didn't know if I felt comfortable sharing certain aspects of myself with the world. I'm not good at being vulnerable, which is essentially what my blog had to be if it was going to be good.

Ultimately I decided to launch TheBaysics.com speaking on topics such as professional navigation, taking risks, being Black, and using my own personal experiences. It was real and it was raw. If more people shared their trials and tribulations in life showing that imperfection is more normal than perfection, I think a lot more of us would start making decisions solely for ourselves. I've become more confident in the person I am knowing it was those trials that make me the person I am today.

I think a lot of people associate a level of vainness around loving one's self. I previously dated a guy who would look at himself in the mirror every few seconds while we had sex. He worked out twice a day and was super conscious about the foods he put in his body. He was proud of his physical accomplishments. Seeing photos of him from previous years, I could tell that he had definitely made quite the transformation. While this would offend some women, I'd say to him "Wow, you really love yourself, huh?" in a joking kind of tone. He'd respond and say, "No, you really love yourself!"

While I did love to poke fun at him about this, it was one of the reasons why I liked him so much. He was confident, and that may have been the reason why he liked me as well. We both had "this is me, take it or leave it mentalities." We were both confident in who we were individually. How can you expect for someone to love you, if you don't love yourself? I don't know if I could have said this three or five years ago or even a year ago, but I can honestly say that today's me loves who I am, inside and out.

Take a moment to list out all of the things you love about you, starting each sentence with the words "I love how." Try to speak to both the physical and non-physical aspects of you. Here's my list of things I love about me:

- I love how outspoken I am.

- I love how even though I have big feet they are sample size.

- I love that I can be wrong but loud at the same time.

- I love how ride or die I am for my real friends.

- I love how I fight for what I believe in.

- I love how well my bullshit detector works.

- I love how business savvy I am.

- I love how my breasts look (in which I paid for).

- I love how muscular my legs are.

- I love how my appearance sometimes makes it hard for

people to guess what my heritage is.

· I love how I know my worth.

Now loving yourself isn't just about hyping yourself up about how great you are. It's about acknowledging the things you also need to work on and your imperfections. Do the same thing you did above but this time start each sentence with "I need to work on." Here's my list of things I am working on:

· I need to work on giving people a chance before writing them off.

· I need to work on better understanding other people's point of views.

· I need to work on my insecurities around my stretch marks.

· I need to work on being vulnerable while dating.

· I need to work on my ego.

· I need to work on being more patient in the workplace.

· I need to work on keeping a tidier room.

· I need to work on not wanting to go off on every girl that pushes me or gives me a dirty look at the bar.

· I need to work on not assuming someone is talking badly about me when they stare at me.

· I need to work on being more involved in the community.

· I need to work on consistently bringing lunch to work.

If this was a difficult exercise for you, that's perfectly OK. Loving yourself takes time and practice. Be patient while discovering the undiscovered aspects of you.

Using the space below, write out
five things you love about yourself.

1.

2.

3.

4.

5.

Using the space below, write out five things
you would like to work on about yourself.

1.

2.

3.

4.

5.

CHAPTER ELEVEN

Your "Did I Choose The Right Career Path" Battle

Have you ever heard the term "quarter life crisis"? According to Merideth Goldstein of The Boston Globe,

The quarter-life crisis occurs in one's twenties, after entering the real world. Common symptoms of a quarter-life crisis are often feelings of being "lost,scared, lonely or confused" about what steps to take to transition properly into adulthood. Studies have shown

that unemployment and choosing a career path is a major cause for young persons to undergo stress or anxiety. Early stages of one living on their own for the first time and learning to cope without parental help can also induce feelings of isolation and loneliness. Re-evaluation of one's close personal relationships can also be a factor, with sufferers feeling they have outgrown their partner or believing others may be more suitable for them.[2]

If I had to put money on it, I'd say almost everyone this day and age has either experienced, still experiencing, or will experience the symptoms described above. Whether you're still in college and second guessing the major you chose or four years graduated and hating your current job, we all will experience that moment where you're self reflecting on your life and second guessing decisions you have made. I have good and bad news for you.

The bad news?

2. (Source: Wikipedia. https://en.wikipedia.org/wiki/Quarter-life_crisis. Accessed October 25, 2019.)

There is absolutely no way for any of us to change the past. There's no amount of money. There's no amount of social status. We're all given the same amount of time in a day. 24 hours. 1,440 minutes. 86,400 seconds.

The good news?

We are still so young! We can change and shape our future! Make a plan to get to where you want to be. Take risks. For those of you who have no kids, this is the time in your life where the risks you make have the smallest level of impact on others. No one is dependent on you.

If you want to travel, go fucking travel. Save money. Find a remote from home job.

If you want to start a business, create a business plan. Attend free seminars that other entrepreneurs host. Find investors. Get a loan.

I mentored a girl from Florida State a few years after I graduated. One day she called me crying because she hated the major she chose. She didn't have the money to switch majors because it would require her to stay an additional year and a half. She was a retail merchandising major and had realized midway into her major that public relations is what she really wanted to do. After asking her to get it together, I explained to her that in most job fields, no one cares about what you majored in as long as you have experience. I told her

to continue in her major and to put
her energy into finding part-time public relations internship
during school.

I have friends who are five years into their careers who are not
happy with what they're doing in life. While we're discovering
what we like and what we are good at, we're discovering what
we don't like, too. Every job is an experience and we have to
remember to apply these learnings going forward. If we are not
learning, we're just going to be stuck in this feeling of having no
purpose. I remembered a low point I had hit towards the end of
my stint in Seattle. I shared this feeling only with my parents. I was
embarrassed to tell anyone else. One day I said to a close friend,
"I'm not sure if this is what I'm supposed to be doing in life."

I had never said anything like this to her before. Her response?

"Girl, I have those thoughts every day." I was completely in shock. I
couldn't believe someone else had the same thoughts I had been
having. As I began talking about it with other people, more of my
friends were sharing the same fears of not knowing what they
wanted to do.

So you're probably reading this and are like "OK, can this heifer
hurry up and get to the part where she tells us how to win this
so called battle." If I'm being perfectly transparent, which I've
been from Page 1 (Get it? Day one? Page one?) I'm still fighting
my own, "Did I Choose the Right Career Path" battle. I can say
however, that I'm closer than ever to figuring it out. A few years
ago, I listed out all of the things I looked for in a company and in

my job and to label each one with an N for negotiable or NN for non-negotiable. By using the next figure, I'd like to ask you to do the same.

FIGURE 11

YOUR **IDEAL CAREER**

The following exercise is designed to help you discover the qualities your desire for your ideal career. Using the example below, list your Top 10 negotiables and non-negotiables for your career.

EXAMPLE

NEGOTIABLES (N)	NON-NEGOTIABLES (NN)
1. Ability to Telework	1. Commute Over 30 Minutes
2. Flexible Start Time	2. Limited Vacation Time
3. Office Location	3. Traveling More Than Two Weeks a Month

NEGOTIABLES (N)	NON-NEGOTIABLES (NN)
1.	1.
2.	2.
3.	3.
4.	4.
5.	5.
6.	6.
7.	7.
8.	8.
9.	9.
10.	10.

Once you've created your list, compare it against your current job situation or if you're still in college figure out if the career you are aspiring to get into will give you those things. Remember, the things you labeled as "NN" (non-negotiable) are most important and crucial.

This exercise was super helpful for me because it helped me weed out all the background noise and focus on what's most important to me. It also helped me realize what jobs were not the right fit earlier on.

The "Did I Choose the Right Career Path" battle knows no age, race, and gender. We all go through it, yet we unfortunately don't all find what it is we're looking for. A few weekends ago I had a conversation with a stranger at the bar (something, not unusual for me at all) and we began talking about work. I asked him the question, "Do you love your job?" He said yes so quickly. He didn't even have to think anything over. I want that for me, and I want that for you. I thought to myself, "WOW! What a blessing to be doing something you love." He was only 32. He had what people search for their entire lifetime and sometimes never find. I'm a firm believer that people make time for what's truly important to them and you are the ultimate decider of where you go in life.

The Life Lessons College Failed to Teach You is my torch to you.

We've covered making a budget, interviewing, dating, jobs from hell, unemployment, non-ideal living arrangements, being selfish, and loving yourself.

I now challenge you to not only utilize the torch I am passing, but for you to discuss these topics in your everyday life, whether it's with your peers, your family, close friends, or younger students you may mentor.

Be more open about your trials and tribulations so that others can learn from your mistakes. Don't let you or your friends get distracted by your followers' "perfect" Instagram lives. Encourage others to not settle and to search endlessly for their happiness.

So what are you waiting on?

Go make a plan, take strategic risks, learn from your [inevitable] mistakes, help others, and most importantly, put your happiness first because if you don't, no one else will.

ACKNOWLEDGEMENTS

My deepest gratitude goes to

God, you have continuously opened doors for me financially, personally, and professionally.

Judy Gitenstein, you have been the most amazing resource from the very beginning. Thank you for taking a twenty something year old seriously even when they knew absolutely nothing about writing a book. You have given me insight on the ins and outs of the industry, you have provided thought provoking writing advice, and you have provided me with connections that I would have not been able to make on my own.

Jarryd Boyd, you have been one of my biggest cheerleaders and not to mention, a pro bono public relations consultant throughout this entire process. You have continuously allowed me to use so many of your talents, skills, and limited free time to make this book happen.

Cheryl Edwards, my dear old friend that I am so lucky to have! You were the first set of eyes (other than mine) who read my unfinished manuscript in its very early stages. Your thoughts and positive encouragement was the push I needed to pursue publishing and to actually invest in myself further.

Brenda Heald, my developmental editing hero. Your editing pushed me to think of different ways I could take my book to the ultimate next level.

Last but not least, Leah Lakins, a Chief Creative Officer Book Champion. The moment I hired you I knew my book would finally see the light of day. You have turned an idea I had in 2015 into an actual reality for me.

Made in the USA
Middletown, DE
23 November 2019

79290772R00111